D1594787

The Highland Battles

Warfare on Scotland's Northern Frontier in the Early Middle Ages

Chris Peers

Pen & Sword
MILITARY

First published in Great Britain in 2020 by
Pen & Sword Military
An imprint of
Pen & Sword Books Ltd
Yorkshire – Philadelphia

ISBN 978 1 52674 174 5

A CIP catalogue record for this book is
available from the British Library.

Typeset by Mac Style
Printed and bound in the UK by TJ Book Limited,
Padstow, Cornwall.

Pen & Sword Books Limited incorporates the imprints of Atlas,
Archaeology, Aviation, Discovery, Family History, Fiction, History,
Maritime, Military, Military Classics, Politics, Select, Transport,
True Crime, Air World, Frontline Publishing, Leo Cooper, Remember
When, Seaforth Publishing, The Praetorian Press, Wharncliffe
Local History, Wharncliffe Transport, Wharncliffe True Crime
and White Owl.

For a complete list of Pen & Sword titles please contact

PEN & SWORD BOOKS LIMITED
47 Church Street, Barnsley, South Yorkshire, S70 2AS, England
E-mail: enquiries@pen-and-sword.co.uk
Website: www.pen-and-sword.co.uk

Or

PEN AND SWORD BOOKS
1950 Lawrence Rd, Havertown, PA 19083, USA
E-mail: Uspen-and-sword@casematepublishers.com
Website: www.penandswordbooks.com

Contents

Acknowledgments

The author would like to thank the following for their assistance:

VisitScotland, and especially the advisors at Bowmore, Inverness and Stornoway.

The very helpful staff at Caithness Horizons, Thurso, and the Visitor Centre at Burghead.

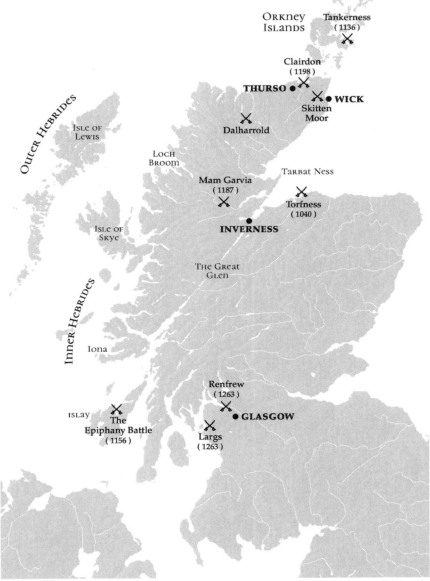

A map of Scotland, based on J.H. Colton's map of 1855, showing the locations of the battlefields featured in this book:

1. Skitten Moor, Caithness, ninth and tenth century AD.
2. Torfness (Burghead), Moray, 1040.
3. Tankerness, Orkney, 1136.
4. Renfrew (Braehead), 1164.
5. Mam Garvia (Strath Garve), Easter Ross, 1187.
6. Clairdon (Thurso), Caithness, 1198.
7. Largs, Ayrshire, 1263.

Introduction

Scotland is a country that is visited by millions every year, attracted by its breathtaking scenery, the tranquillity of its wild places and the hospitality and vibrant culture of its people, but also by its history. At sites like Edinburgh and Stirling castles, and the battlefields at Bannockburn and Culloden, visitors can be entertained and educated with well-designed exhibitions, re-enactments and even computer simulations evoking the great events that have taken place on those very spots. But especially in the north and west of the country, countless other battlefields, and the dramatic stories that they recall, remain almost unknown.

Nevertheless, although there may be no monuments or visitor centres, there has often been no archaeological investigation, and the exact location of the site may not even be evident on the ground, there is still much to be learned from studying the terrain in conjunction with the contemporary written sources describing the events that occurred there. The seven battles and associated campaigns discussed in this book are just a small selection from this great untapped resource. They have been chosen because they help to fill in some of the gaps in popular understanding of Scotland's history, but also because together they tell an important part of the story of mediaeval Scotland. Some of the sites are worth visiting just for their isolation and beauty. At Tankerness, for example, the dominant sounds are still the calls of the oystercatcher, skylark and curlew, just as they must have been on the day, nearly 900 years ago, when the Hebridean fleet sailed into the sound to confront the men of Orkney. Others, like

Renfrew, where the great Somerled met his death in 1164, have almost disappeared under modern development. But I have visited them all, walked the ground and, I hope, learned something new about the events that took place there. Scotland is a small country with a good transport infrastructure and none of the sites are particularly difficult to reach, so each chapter concludes with a brief survey of what there is to see today, with grid references and directions for those interested enough to make the journey.

Setting the scene

The theme that links these seven battles is the three-sided confrontation which took place on the northern and western frontiers of Scotland in the early Middle Ages: the period between the first Viking settlements in the ninth century AD, and the establishment of royal authority over the Gaelic-speaking inhabitants of the west of the country by the kings of Scots during the thirteenth and fourteenth century. The territory over which the fleets and armies of these different powers manoeuvred and fought corresponds roughly to what are known today as the 'Highlands and Islands' of Scotland. The exceptions are the two battles at Renfrew in 1164 and Largs in 1263, both of which were fought south of the River Clyde, in the area generally referred to as the Central Lowlands, but pitted local Scottish forces against invaders coming from the nearby Western Isles.

The generally accepted definition of 'the Highlands' incorporates the entire Scottish mainland north and west of the Highland Line or Highland Boundary Fault, a geological fault line which runs from the mouth of the River Clyde on the Atlantic coast north-east to Stonehaven on the North Sea about 15 miles south of the city of Aberdeen (Darling & Boyd, 1964). Beyond that line the terrain is generally more mountainous and the soils poorer than further south, but there is some good agricultural land to be found along the east coast, and even inland the nature of the country differs dramatically from one sub-region to another. To simplify matters, the Highlands are themselves divided by another fault line, the Great Glen, which also runs from south-west to north-east, and is marked by a string of water features including lochs Linnhe and Ness. (It may be worth pointing out here, for those unfamiliar with the country, that the term 'loch' is applied both to freshwater lakes like Loch Ness and to inlets of the sea like Loch Linnhe, some of which – on the west coast in particular – are long and narrow enough to recall the fjords of Norway.) South and east of the Great Glen the interior consists of relatively gentle and rounded hills, the remains of an enormous plateau ground down by glaciers during the Ice Ages. In the north the hills give way to an extensive and well-populated coastal plain fringing the southern shore of the Moray Firth. In mediaeval times the name Moray, now restricted to a section of this plain, was applied to the majority of the south-eastern Highland region. The land of Moray will feature prominently in our story, although only one of the seven battles featured, Torfness in 1040, was actually fought there.

Not technically part of Moray, but sharing many of its characteristics, is the region on the other side of the Great Glen around the western and northern shores of the Moray Firth, which is known today as Easter Ross. This area possessed a resource that all the districts further north and west lacked: timber of sufficient size and quality for shipbuilding. This was especially the case since Norse shipbuilding techniques relied on carving planks into shape with axes rather than sawing them, and were consequently notoriously wasteful of timber. The shortage of large trees in the northern mainland and its neighbouring islands is not due to latitude: there are substantial forests in Norway, nearly ten degrees further north. But poor soils and exposure to constant wind mean that trees of a height and girth suitable for making ships were not to be found beyond Strath Oykel and the Dornoch Firth in Easter Ross, on the south-eastern border of what is now the county of Sutherland. (The word 'strath', like 'glen', denotes a valley, but the former is usually wider and more suitable for farming.) Ships were often built in Norway for export to the Norse settlers in the Orkney and Shetland isles, but the forests along the River Oykel and further south in Ross were a valuable strategic resource for the earls of Orkney, and one which repeatedly encouraged them to push south into territory occupied or claimed by the Scots.

West of the Great Glen lie the districts of Badenoch, Lochaber and Wester Ross. Here the ice has cut more deeply into the land, leaving behind a country of steep mountains and knife-edge ridges separated by narrow glens or valleys. The mountains intercept the moist winds coming from the Atlantic Ocean, and the consequent high rainfall, rather than assisting agriculture, leaches what nutrients there are from the soil and encourages the formation of peat bogs. The difficulty of travelling through this terrain earned it the alternative name of Garmoran, or the 'Rough Bounds', and a reputation as a hideout of rebels and outlaws, many of whom succeeded in defying the kings of Scots until the end of the sixteenth century. Again only one of our battles took place here, on the eastern fringe of the region, at Mam Garvia in 1187.

Further north, in Sutherland and Caithness, the glaciers lingered longer and only the oldest and hardest rocks survived the process of erosion. Here isolated peaks, often carved into fantastic shapes, stand out in isolation from a landscape of bogs, small lochs and bare rock, interrupted by the occasional habitable 'strath' like that of the River Naver in northern Sutherland. Although the average altitude here is less than further south, the latitude and the lack of good soil make it no less difficult a place to earn a living. The exception is Caithness, at the far north-eastern tip of the Scottish mainland, where the vagaries of geology have exposed a layer of sandstone which weathers easily to produce fertile soil, and incidentally also makes an excellent building material. Rainfall is also more moderate here than further west, allowing arable crops like oats and barley to be grown, while the long hours of daylight in the growing season contribute to the production of excellent grass for grazing livestock. In fact tributes and rents in Caithness, and the neighbouring Orkney Isles off the north coast, were traditionally paid in the form of the abundant butter produced by their great herds of cattle. It is therefore not surprising that Orkney and Caithness were relatively densely populated as early as Neolithic times, nor that when the Scandinavians began their expansion overseas in the eighth century AD these were the areas that attracted their first settlements. Because people were concentrated here, so was warfare; three of our battle sites – at Skitten Moor, Clairdon and Tankerness – are to be found in Caithness and Orkney.

The Orkneys, and the Shetland Isles further north, both consist of a cluster of islands surrounding the largest, which in both cases is known rather confusingly as Mainland. They are traditionally excluded from what are known as the Hebrides, the Western Isles, or simply the Isles. The latter comprise not only the countless islands of the Inner Hebrides just off the west coast, of which the largest – from north to south – are Skye, Mull, Jura and Islay, but also the long archipelago of the Outer Hebrides further west, which stretches over 120 miles from the Butt of Lewis in the north to the little island of Berneray in the south. The Western Isles are extremely diverse. Along some of the exposed western coasts of the Outer Hebrides the acidity of the soil is counteracted by the lime-rich shell sand blown inland from the beaches to produce a long, narrow strip of good grazing, or 'machair', while the east coasts and the interior are largely dominated by peat bogs. Islay is low lying and fertile and was the headquarters of many of the warlords who fought to control the Isles, while neighbouring Jura is mountainous and less productive. But if much of the land in the islands was of little value for farming, in the early Middle Ages this was compensated for by their situation on the trade routes which grew up between Scandinavia and its outposts in Orkney and Caithness on the one hand, and Ireland and western Britain on the other. And the greatest export of the Hebrides was its people, who had a well-deserved reputation as ferocious warriors. If none of the battles featured in these pages actually took place there, Hebrideans fought with distinction in all of them.

The shortage of good land meant that, with the few exceptions exemplified by the barley fields of Caithness and Orkney, the economy of the Highlands and Islands was based mainly on cattle rather than agriculture. Many of the people were therefore semi-nomadic, moving with their beasts between the high mountain pastures in the summer and the more sheltered coastal villages in winter. Low population densities meant that wild animals were abundant, and the red deer in particular was a prized source of meat, just as it is today. This part-pastoral and part-hunting lifestyle was alien to the Highlanders' southern neighbours, and especially to the Anglo-Normans whose influence at the Scottish court became predominant from the late eleventh century onwards. Consequently the Lowlanders developed a tendency to regard the Highlanders – and the Galwegians of the south-west, whose culture and economy were similar – as barbarians. By the time John of Fordun wrote his *Chronica Gentis Scottorum* or *Chronicles of the Scottish Nation* in the fourteenth century, this prejudice was being intensified by a growing language barrier, as the Gaelic tongue, which had once been spoken even at the royal court, gradually retreated beyond the Highland Line.

Gaelic was a Celtic language closely related to Irish, and so is generally supposed to have been introduced by the Scots of Dal Riata, in present-day Argyll in the south-west Highlands, whose ruling class had migrated from Ireland around the year 500 AD (Jackson, 1953). In fact archaeology does not support the idea of a large-scale migration at this time, so it is possible that Gaelic speakers had been present in the west for much longer. In any case the language had spread to most of the rest of Scotland following the establishment of a royal dynasty descended from the kings of Dal Riata under Kenneth MacAlpin in the 840s. In the process it supplanted the language of the previous inhabitants of the Highlands and Islands, the Picts. The name of this people is derived from a Latin term meaning painted or tattooed, and first appears in the context of a confederation of anti-Roman tribes in northern Britain in the last decade of the third century AD. We do not know what the Picts called themselves, but their language is believed to have been related to Old Welsh, another branch of the Celtic tongues which were probably spoken across most of Britain in the Iron Age. A notable exception to the dominance of Gaelic was Orkney and the north-east of Caithness, where it appears that the language had not arrived before the Scandinavians took over, so that Pictish was replaced directly by dialects of Old Norse.

Kenneth MacAlpin (mac Alpin) was the son of Alpin, ruler of Dal Riata, and a Pictish princess, and the unification of the Picts and Scots into what became known as the Scottish kingdom is traditionally ascribed to him. It is misleading, however, to think of the Picts as having been replaced by the Scots, still less exterminated. The merger of the two peoples seems to have been achieved fairly peacefully; the new king is said to have treacherously killed seven earls who might have disputed his right to rule, but there was nothing particularly unusual in this in the context of early mediaeval Scottish history. The new 'nation' (to use an anachronistic term) took the name of Kenneth's father's people, the Scots of Argyll, but its true power base was in the former Pictish heartland, in the lower lying, more productive and more densely populated east of the country. In fact, throughout the Middle Ages and beyond Scotland was, in the words of Professor Barrow, 'a North Sea country' (Barrow, 1992). Its trade was with England and the countries of Western Europe beyond the North Sea, and the bulk of the fertile agricultural land was in the east. For most of our period towns were restricted almost exclusively to the east coast and the river valleys which flowed towards it. But beyond the mountainous central spine of the country the cultural links of the inhabitants continued to point in different directions.

The Western Isles maintained close connections with Ireland, from where men came to fight as allies or mercenaries in several of the battles described here. Further north, the Outer Hebrides, Orkney and Shetland had already been occupied by seafarers from Norway by the time Kenneth MacAlpin came to power, and possibly a generation earlier. In fact it is likely that the Viking onslaught helped to secure Kenneth's succession by destabilising the old power centre of the northern Picts around Inverness. But whatever the situation in the northern isles, and possibly the far north-eastern tip of Caithness where Norse place names similarly prevail (see Chapter 2), the Gaelic-speaking population of most of the mainland and the Hebrides remained in place, and over time gave rise to a mixed Norse-Celtic society whose members came to be known by the Gaelic name of 'Gall Gaidhil' or 'foreign Gaels'. The extent of this mixing is suggested by the fact that Scottish Gaelic shows strong signs of Scandinavian influence, and compared to its close cousin Irish it has evidently undergone a process of grammatical simplification at some point in its history (Jackson, 1953). This is often the mark of a language which was widely adopted by people for whom it was not their native tongue – in this case assimilated Vikings.

So the story of the battles described in this book is really three stories, depending on one's perspective. From Bergen in Norway, or Kirkwall in Orkney, it might be seen as part of the story of the rise and fall of Norway's seaborne empire, beginning with the settlement of Orkney and Caithness, battles won against the Picts and Scots, and then a long defensive struggle by the Earls of Orkney against the growing power of the Scottish kings, culminating in Norway's final abandonment of the Hebrides after the Battle of Largs in 1263. From the Gaelic-speaking lands on Scotland's northern and western periphery the history of the Middle Ages is that of the gradual retreat and ultimate destruction of a culture, the start of a long trail that would end in the proscription of the Gaelic language itself after the Battle of Culloden in 1746. On the other hand, from a lowland perspective, this is the story of the building of a Scottish nation, featuring the growing power of a line of heroic kings, from Malcolm Canmore to William the Lion, who gradually extended their authority from their old heartland in the south-east as far as the Atlantic Ocean, and so laid the foundations of the kingdom which would so stoutly defend its freedom from the English in the fourteenth century.

Chapter 1

The Men and the Weapons

Recruitment and military organisation

In order to help make sense of the campaigns discussed below without excessive repetition or long digressions from the narrative, it may be useful to begin by looking at the kinds of men and armies which took part in them. We have frustratingly little information on how early Scottish forces were raised or equipped, but to simplify a little, there were four ways of raising a force of fighting men. Probably the most ancient was what in the later Middle Ages was termed 'Scottish' or 'Common Army' service. This was based on the principle that all free men were liable to be called up by their rulers for the defence of the country, although in practice it usually took the form of a quota of soldiers imposed on each territorial unit in proportion to its size or population. An early if controversial source for this kind of service is a Gaelic document known as the *Miniugud Senchasa Fher nAlban*, or *Genealogy of the Men of Alba*, which was written in the tenth century, but seems originally to have referred to the period around the year 700 (Foster, 2014). It purports to give a breakdown of military service owed to the kings of Dal Riata in Argyll. Groups of houses – usually between twenty and thirty – are listed, together with the numbers of men and boats which they were supposed to supply.

Each group of twenty houses was apparently responsible for two seven-bench rowing vessels, which, allowing two rowers to a bench, implies a total of around thirty crewmen. On that basis Argyll might have raised around 2,000 fighting men altogether (Heath, 1980), but the document does not explain what proportion of the total population was liable for call-up, so we do not know whether this figure represents a mass levy or a more selective muster, perhaps on the basis of a hereditary obligation or property qualification. Neither can we be sure that the system was ever extended to the rest of the kingdom, even after its unification under Kenneth MacAlpin, although its similarity to the later system of Scottish service suggests some sort of continuity. In the Common Army as documented in the thirteenth and fourteenth centuries, the quota of men enlisted varied according to circumstances, usually between one and three per 'davoch' or 'ploughshare', though at one point King Robert the Bruce demanded the attendance of every man prosperous enough to own a cow, which especially in the Highlands must have been almost everyone. Local contingents were commanded by royal appointees, who were known as late as the twelfth century by the Anglo-Saxon name of 'thanes', while the forces of each earldom were led by its earl.

In earlier centuries the nearest equivalent to the earls were the 'mormaers', officials whose role is discussed further in Chapter 2. In several of the early battles discussed in this book it is likely that the 'Scottish' forces were in fact led by earls or mormaers operating independently of the monarchy, although their forces were presumably raised on similar principles to those levied by the king. Service was normally for only forty days, which naturally limited the effectiveness of the army; in 1215, for example, King Alexander II was forced to raise the siege of Norham in Northumbria after this time and send his Common Army troops home.

Armies raised by this sort of mass levy could be substantial in numbers; the Scottish armies commanded by their kings at major battles against the English like the Standard and Bannockburn probably exceeded 10,000 men, although it is unlikely that those deployed on the northern and western frontiers ever surpassed half that number. But inevitably their standard of training and equipment would be uneven, as most men would have had little or no combat experience, and were often not able to afford the most up-to-date weapons and armour. In 1315, in the aftermath of his victory at Bannockburn, Robert the Bruce attempted to standardise the equipment of the Common Army, decreeing for example that each man possessing property worth ten pounds or more should provide himself with a sword and a spear, as well as an aketon or padded coat, a helmet and gauntlets, while wealthier men would also have a coat of mail (Heath, 1982). Even at that period, however, there must have been many soldiers who were less well protected, like those illustrated on the famous Carlisle Charter of 1316 (Reid, 2013), which shows that town under siege by Scotsmen who appear to lack any sort of armour and wear only shirts and cloaks.

In Orkney and other areas under Norse rule a similar arrangement to the Common Army service was introduced, apparently based on the Norwegian 'leidang'. Under this system men were obliged to serve for up to four months a year, either on land or as part of the crew of a warship. In Orkney in the later Middle Ages the land was divided into units called ouncelands, each of which represented the nominal value of an ounce of silver. An ounceland was subdivided into eighteen pennylands, which were probably equivalent to a single farm. We do not know the date that this system was introduced, but Crawford (2013) believes that the ouncelands at least were in existence very early in the history of the earldom, although the subdivision into pennylands was probably an innovation introduced in the eleventh century by Earl Thorfinn the Mighty (see Chapter 3). The relationship of this system to that of military recruitment is not certain, but it has been calculated that with a total of 216 ouncelands, each liable to provide four men for the leidang, the Orkney Isles alone would have raised a total of around 800 men and sixteen large ships (Heath, 1982, presumably following H. Marwick, whose theory was based on fourteenth-century documents). A similar arrangement seems to have been introduced into Caithness, although it is poorly documented and was replaced by the Scottish system of ploughshares at a fairly early date. In the Hebrides the ouncelands were known by the Gaelic term 'tirunga' and were divided into 20 pennylands each, but the principle was presumably very similar, and it is likely that the system was introduced there by the earls of Orkney. We also know that many of the better-off Orkney farmers retained a degree of independence, and especially in the civil wars between the earls they were free to either choose a side or remain aloof altogether, based on calculations of their own self-interest. Earl Sigurd the Stout, for example, was obliged to restore the land rights of the farmers, which had been lost under one of his predecessors, in order to secure their loyalty in the face of an attack on Caithness (see Chapter 2). Before the Battle of Tankerness in 1136 (Chapter 4) Earl Paul sent out messengers in haste to gather men overnight in the face of an unexpected threat, and found the next day that he had more volunteers than he had expected, in fact more than he could fit on his ships. One local farmer, Erlend of Tankerness, offered his help on the morning of the battle, but was set to gathering rocks on the beach for use as missiles because there was nowhere for him and his followers to deploy.

Most armies operating in the north, however, were probably smaller but better equipped than the rank and file of the Common Army or the leidang. James Fraser (2012) argues that in most of Britain between the sixth and eleventh centuries AD campaigns were fought mainly by small bands of professional warriors, the more or less full-time retinues of kings and nobles. Such men would probably be well protected by mail body armour and iron helmets, and well trained in the use of weapons such as the sword, axe and bow. Most of the evidence for this comes from the Anglo-Saxon kingdoms of England, but it is also likely to have been the case among the Picts and Scots.

Certainly the forty mounted men who accompanied Maelbrigte to his encounter with Earl Sigurd the Mighty (see Chapter 2) must have been just such a picked elite. In the later Middle Ages Highland clan chiefs were accompanied in battle by bodyguard units known in Gaelic as '*luchd-taighe*' or '*teaglach*', both of which mean something like 'household'. Traditionally these units were very small, no more than twelve men strong (Fraser, 2012). We do not know whether similar bodyguards existed in our period, though the ease with which their enemies managed not only to kill but subsequently to decapitate Somerled and Donald Ban MacWilliam (see Chapters 5 and 6) suggests that if they did they were not very effective. In the Norse territories such retinues were often not much bigger; according to *Orkneyinga Saga*, for example, the combined force which the joint earls Rognvald and Harald led to Forsie in Caithness in 1158 comprised only 100 foot and twenty horse. (And once again they failed to protect Rognvald, who met his death there.) On the other hand, of course, a force which was made up of experienced full-time fighters, well motivated and lavishly equipped at their leader's expense, could in theory be effective out of all proportion to its numbers. Fraser points out that in contrast to the situation in Ireland, Highlands and Islands forces in the later Middle Ages did not include a significant number of mounted troops, probably because of their reliance on seaborne transport as well as a shortage of suitable grazing in the coastal lands of the west. Elsewhere Scottish armies were often well mounted on native ponies, large enough to transport an infantryman to the battlefield, if not to carry a fully armoured knight in a charge. However Maelbrigte's forty mounted followers are evidence that in earlier times, when cavalry equipment was lighter, these locally bred animals may actually have been ridden into battle.

A third source of troops for all the armies operating on the northern and western frontiers of Scotland came from volunteers and mercenaries, whom we might define as all those for whom war was a business enterprise rather than a defensive expedient or a legal or social obligation. We often read in *Orkneyinga Saga* of the earls of Orkney raising troops in the Hebrides and Ireland, and their example seems to have been followed by the MacWilliam rebels in the late twelfth century (see Chapter 6). The Western Isles were difficult places to make a living, and for many of their young men, underemployed at home but familiar with ships and the sea, a career as a pirate or a soldier of fortune offered the easiest way to riches. In the later Middle Ages the Isles were the source of the gallowglasses (Gaelic '*gall oglaigh*' or 'foreign warriors') who campaigned in Ireland as mercenary warriors and bodyguards, and their predecessors appeared on most of the battlefields under discussion here, although the terms on which they served are not recorded. Less well equipped were the '*cethern*' or '*caterans*', landless mercenaries of lower status than the gallowglasses and probably serving for a share of plunder rather than for pay. They earned a reputation for rapaciousness and indiscipline in the armies of men like Alexander Stewart, the 'Wolf of Badenoch', in the fourteenth century, and their ancestors may have been an essential part of Scottish armies in our era. Also in this category were those Norsemen who retained the traditions of their Viking ancestors and combined farming with raiding, either on their own behalf or as part of the following of a more powerful leader. The better off among these men might employ their own retinues of retainers. A famous passage in *Orkneyinga Saga* describes the routine of the notorious Svein Asleifsson of Gairsay as late as the 1160s:

This was how Svein used to live. Winter he would spend at home on Gairsay, where he entertained some eighty men at his own expense... In the spring he had more than enough to occupy him, with a great deal of seed to sow which he saw to carefully himself. Then when that job was done, he would go off plundering in the Hebrides and Ireland on what he called his 'spring trip', then back home just after mid-summer, where stayed till the cornfields had been reaped and the grain was safely in. After that he would go off raiding again, and never came back till the first month of winter was ended. This he used to call his 'autumn trip'.

From as early as the reign of MacBeth (1040 to 1057) the Scottish kings were also employing mercenary Norman cavalry. Even before their conquest of England in 1066 the Normans had earned a reputation throughout Europe as formidable warriors, thanks to the impact of their close-order cavalry charges using sword and lance. Just as useful in Scottish conditions was their ability to fight on foot, protected by large kite-shaped shields and increasingly comprehensive coats of mail. Anglo-Norman knights could even attain high office in the service of the Scottish crown; for example, the victor of the Battle of Stracathro against the rebellious lords of Moray in 1130 was the Constable of Scotland, an Englishman named Edward Siwardsson, whose duties specifically included commanding the knights of the *'familia regis'*, or royal household. But the number of mercenaries available was always limited, and during the twelfth century the Scottish kings began to introduce feudal service on the same lines as that in England and the rest of Western Europe. David I is widely credited with this idea, but there is evidence that feudalisation had begun before his reign, and it was certainly not complete in the north for a long time afterwards (Oram, 2008). Under this system the monarch granted land to his vassals in return for the service of a specified number of soldiers. These might be knights, fully armed and mounted on expensive war horses, or sergeants, who also served on horseback but whose armour was generally lighter and their equipment less lavish. This difference was reflected in the value of the land grants, which for a sergeant was roughly a quarter of that required to maintain a knight. Many of these grants were to individual knights or sergeants, but some prominent men were expected to provide larger contingents, either by subinfeudation – letting part of their lands to subordinate knights on similar terms to those on which they held theirs from the king – or by maintaining their own retinues of full-time retainers. For example, in the reign of David I Robert de Brus held Annandale in return for the service of ten knights.

In many cases this new knightly class was recruited from among local magnates like Earl Duncan of Fife, whose earldom was in effect transformed by David into a feudal fief in 1136, (Strickland, 2012), but other fiefs were granted to immigrants from England or elsewhere in Europe. One of the most successful of these at the time was a Flemish nobleman named Freskin, who was first granted lands in Lothian early in the reign of David I, then received further grants in Moray, apparently in the aftermath of the victory at Stracathro, as part of a policy of replacing the rebellious local magnates with men whose loyalty could be relied on. Freskin's descendants went on to build on his power base in the north and found the families of Murray (originally 'de Moravia' or 'of Moray') and Sutherland. Other newcomers whose families went on to have prominent roles in Scottish history included Robert de Brus of Annandale, ancestor of the Bruces, and Walter Fitz Alan, first High Steward of Scotland under David, whose descendants later took the name of Stewart or Stuart. According to one view the effect of this policy of feudalisation was to divide the kingdom rather than strengthen it, because the imposition of an alien social system and the influx of these favoured outsiders were unpopular in the Gaelic north and west, and this may have been an important motive in the rebellions of men like Somerled and the MacWilliams (chapters 5 and 6). Conversely, the Scottish kings were now able to raise a fighting force which could take on the English knights on equal terms. The overall numbers of such knights, however, remained relatively small: at the Battle of the Standard in 1138, for example, there were only 200 of them, and although David's son Henry led them in a charge which broke through the English line, they were too few to influence the course of the fighting and were forced to retreat. Strickland suggests that even in the thirteenth century the number of 'heavy cavalry' – presumably including similarly equipped sergeants as well as knights – 'probably rarely exceeded the low hundreds'.

Military costume in the Early Middle Ages

What would the armies of the period have looked like? There is not much evidence for how Scottish troops of the time were dressed, but Pictish stone carvings appear to show men in long shirts and overgarments which might be hooded cloaks, cloaks with separate hoods like those worn in much of medieval Europe, or perhaps early plaids pulled over the head. The fourteenth-century Carlisle Charter shows the town being besieged by Scotsmen wearing very similar costumes, shod but barelegged, with their shirts tied between their legs and hoods over their heads. It is therefore reasonable to assume that similar attire was also typical of the intervening centuries. In earlier times, when metal armour was less widely available, such unprotected men seem to have been the norm, and it was common for the better-armed English knights to mock the Scots for their near nakedness. The chronicler Ailred of Rievaulx, for example, quotes Walter Espec in his speech before the Battle of the Standard as assuring his Norman knights that they had nothing to fear from 'the worthless Scot with half naked buttocks'. This lack of conventional clothing was not then restricted to the Highlanders with whom it was associated in later times; the besiegers of Carlisle had probably been recruited locally in the Borders, while the troops at the Standard appear to have come from Galloway and Lothian. The question of the origins of what are now thought of as specifically Highland items of dress remains controversial, but the ninth-century

Drosten Stone near Arbroath, in Angus, shows a figure in a typical Pictish hooded cloak, which may represent an early version of what eventually became the tartan plaid. Diodorus Siculus, writing in the first century BC, describes the Gauls as wearing mantles patterned in 'small squares of many colours', a phrase echoed by the sixteenth-century commentator George Buchanan a millennium and a half later (Reid, 2013). The ancestors of the Highlanders of his day, Buchanan tells us, wore 'plaids of many colours', their favourites being purple and blue. The famous saffron-dyed war shirt, or '*leine croich*', which was associated with Highland and Irish warriors in the later Middle Ages, does not appear to have been in use in our period. Neither do we have any evidence from this era of specific clan tartans, but it is reasonable to suppose that localities would differ in the availability of dyes and the traditional patterns used for weaving, so that it might have been possible to guess at a man's place of origin from his dress, as Martin Martin tells us was the case in the seventeenth century (Reid, 2013), or at least to tell friend from foe.

The Lewis chessmen

By the eleventh century at the latest Norse influence had spread widely through northern and western Scotland, and this is likely to have affected the way the fighting men dressed. Fashions could also move in the opposite direction, however, as is shown by the example of King Magnus Olafsson of Norway, who according to Snorri Sturluson in his *Heimskringla* was nicknamed 'Barelegs', because after his Hebridean campaign of 1098 he and his men abandoned their Scandinavian-style trousers and adopted the local custom of leaving the lower legs and feet bare. This was no doubt a practical arrangement for campaigning in the Isles, where temperatures never fall very low but the ground underfoot is often wet and boggy, so that it is impossible to keep footwear dry. The best-known contemporary evidence for the appearance of twelfth-century islemen consists of the seventy-eight 'Lewis chessmen' which were found on the Isle of Lewis in the early nineteenth century. There were originally reported to have been five more, which subsequently went missing. One of these, a rook, has recently turned up in private hands. (BBC News Scotland, 3 June 2019). These have become some of the most iconic archaeological discoveries in Scottish history, and their images have appeared in numerous books illustrating mediaeval Scottish or Viking warriors. It is therefore worth considering in detail their provenance and their value as a source for our period.

The pieces are mostly carved from walrus ivory, and apart from the pawns they all represent human figures – kings, queens, bishops and soldiers – in the costume of the late twelfth century. The figures average around 10cm in height, and although not quite anatomically realistic they show clothing and equipment in considerable detail. The use of walrus ivory from the Arctic, and stylistic similarities to fragmentary pieces found in Norway, have led nearly all experts to conclude that they were produced in that country, probably in the vicinity of Trondheim (Caldwell et al, 2010). Two key issues for the dating of the pieces are the depiction of the bishops' mitres with the peaks at front and back, rather than at the sides – a style which appeared around 1150 – and the large kite-shaped shields, which are carved showing various patterns but lack the heraldic motifs which were beginning to appear at the end of the twelfth century. They must presumably therefore date from between 1150 and about 1200. The pieces first came to the attention of scholars when they were offered for sale by an Edinburgh antique dealer in 1831; varying accounts of their actual discovery have since emerged, but it is fairly certain that they were found by accident by a farmer on Lewis, either at Camas Uig, near the village of Timsgearraidh on the west coast, or at the site of an old nunnery at Mealasta about six miles further south. The pieces seem to be the survivors of four different chess sets, perhaps the stock of a merchant who had brought them from Norway.

For our purposes the most interesting of the figures are the fifteen knights and thirteen rooks, which have been carved to represent mounted and foot warriors respectively. The knights all wear long coats, which Caldwell et al identify as possibly representing leather armour, though they might equally well be intended to depict surcoats worn over mail. They carry spears or lances as well as shields. Their headgear consists of helmets which are either of the old-fashioned conical type associated with the Vikings and Normans, some apparently with nasals to protect the face, or the more typical late twelfth-century bowl shape. Their horses are modelled as very small in proportion to the riders, and with their long flowing manes they are very reminiscent of the modern Icelandic pony, or the small version of the 'Highland' pony found in the Outer Hebrides. This might be artistic convention, but it might also suggest that the models available to the artist were not knightly cavalry who rode large chargers into combat like the typical European men at arms of the era, but rather men who intended to fight on foot and used such small ponies purely for transport to the battlefield, as was common practice in Scotland. The rooks are similarly equipped to the knights, but are depicted as infantry, each with a kite shield in the left hand and a drawn sword in the right. One figure wears a kettle hat with a prominent brim, and a couple more have helmets of more complex shapes. The shields are decorated with simple geometric designs, mostly featuring crosses. Most of the footsoldiers are wearing similar long coats to those of the mounted men, but three of them have distinctive cross-hatched garments which could be intended to represent mail hauberks. This hypothesis is supported by the description by the Welsh chronicler Gerald de Barri of the Hebrideans at the Battle of Dublin in 1171 as wearing iron armour, which he says was made either of mail, or of small plates or lamellae laced together.

A couple of features depicted on the chessmen appear to be characteristically Scandinavian, although both are rather archaic by twelfth-century standards. Most of the warriors have beards, a fashion which was dying out in Norway by this time, but was still prevalent in the Orkneys and Hebrides, as is witnessed by an allusion in *Sverre's Saga* to the islemen in Sigurd Magnusson's expedition of 1193 as 'island beardies'. And more startlingly, three of the foot figures are shown biting the rims of their shields in a manner reminiscent of the berserkers of the old sagas. It seems unlikely that such behaviour still persisted in real life, nearly two centuries after the arrival of Christianity, but the berserker must still have been an instantly recognisable caricature. In view of the consensus that the pieces originated in Norway, the two aspects of their design that seem to be characteristically Hebridean – the beards and the diminutive ponies – may be coincidence. But that Hebridean and Scandinavian styles of military equipment were essentially the same is confirmed by Gerald de Barri's remark that the islemen at Dublin were armed 'in Danish fashion'. One important difference is that Gerald describes round shields, whereas those depicted on the chessmen are all of the kite-shaped variety, but Ian Heath (1989) suggests that the older round style might have been retained for shipborne campaigns, perhaps as being more suitable for hanging along the sides of a ship. It therefore seems reasonable to take the chessmen as evidence for the general appearance of Hebridean warriors, even if they were not actually carved in the Hebrides. And there may even be a particular local dimension to them, as if they were produced with a specific client in mind. Unfortunately, because as playing pieces they needed to be modelled with wide, flat bases, the infantrymen are depicted with coats or robes descending to the ground, and so it is impossible to tell whether the men who inspired them would have worn Norse-style trousers or breeches, or have followed King Magnus's example and gone into battle barelegged.

The question might be resolved more easily if we knew how the pieces came to be in Lewis, but although there are some unreliable later traditions, we are otherwise reliant on speculation. It has often been supposed that the hoard was buried by a merchant who was en route to the Isle of Man or Ireland, perhaps to preserve it from pirates after an attack or a shipwreck, but Caldwell et al point out that this idea is based on the assumption that Uig was a remote peripheral zone on the edge of the inhabited world. Certainly the district can appear that way today, after centuries of depopulation and the disappearance of the seaborne trade routes between Scandinavia and western Britain which passed through in mediaeval times. In fact, however, it seems to have been one of the main population centres of Lewis in the Viking era and for several centuries afterwards: there is a large pagan-period cemetery at nearby Cnip Headland, while the stronghold of the Macaulay clan in the fourteenth century was at Crowlista overlooking the bay at Uig, and that of the MacLeods was on the island of Great Bernera only six miles to the east. There would therefore have been wealthy individuals living in the area who might have possessed such a luxury item as an ivory chess set, or even commissioned one from a craftsman in Norway. Caldwell quotes a poem in praise of Angus Mor MacDonald, a thirteenth-century descendant of Somerled and a founder of the MacDonald clan, which describes how he inherited a set of chessmen from his father. Angus's headquarters were at Finlaggan on Islay (where Dr Caldwell has excavated what may be the bronze fittings for his dogs' collars), but he is also described as ruling in Lewis. Most of the surviving chessmen are now displayed in the British Museum in London and the National Museum of Scotland in Edinburgh, though individual pieces are regularly lent to other museums, including the Museum nan Eilean in Stornoway on Lewis. There is also a small museum at the presumed site of their discovery at Camas Uig.

Weapons and fighting techniques

It appears that in the early Middle Ages both Highlanders and Lowlanders – in so far as the distinction existed then – were armed with the same mix of weapons. Warriors of the type who might have fought for the northern earls against the Vikings are depicted in the battle scenes on Sueno's Stone, a 23ft-tall carved monument near Forres in Moray which is believed to date from the ninth or tenth century. Some of these men are fighting from horseback with spears, although the figures are too badly eroded to show much detail, and might perhaps resemble the mounted men whom Maelbrigte took to his encounter with Sigurd the Mighty (see Chapter 2). Beneath them are rows of men on foot, armed with spears, swords, possibly bows, and small shields. The stones at Aberlemno in Angus are perhaps a couple of centuries earlier but are better preserved, and confirm that both horse and foot could wear helmets with nasals, and carry round shields and long spears. The prominence of spears is easily understandable. A spear is a fairly cheap and simple weapon to manufacture; it can be used both as a missile weapon and in close combat, and in the latter role its long reach provides a measure of protection for men who might not possess much in the way of defensive armour. Normally wielded one-handed, it also permits its user to protect himself with a shield held in the other hand. Fraser (2012) speculates that the spear may have been the most important missile weapon in Highland warfare until it was supplanted by the bow in the later Middle Ages. It is certainly more commonly mentioned in classic Gaelic poetry, although much Gaelic verse of the time was consciously harking back to the semi-mythical age of Irish epics like the '*Tain Bo Cuailnge*', which is set around the first century AD. The poems do not therefore necessarily reflect the military practice of the period in which they were composed.

A spear can also be wielded in two hands, a method used by Earl Thorfinn at the Battle of Torfness (Chapter 3); this technique is mentioned in several Norse sagas, but is also depicted on one of the probably ninth-century carved stones at Aberlemno, showing that it was known to the Picts even before the Viking invasions. Of course, in order to apply both hands to the spear shaft the warrior would have to either discard his shield, strap it to his wrist if it was small enough, or – as described in *Egil's Saga* – sling it on his back by its carrying strap. Perhaps for this reason the two-handed fighting style often appears in the sagas as a heroic motif, with echoes of the legendary berserkers who went into battle without armour, caring nothing for their own lives and bent purely on slaughter. For example, according to *Egil's Saga* Thorolf Skallagrimsson hacked his way into the enemy lines in this manner at the Battle of Brunanbugh in 937, while *Orkneyinga Saga* insists that Thorfinn 'went ahead of all his troops' at Torfness, and the poet Arnor Thordarsson sang of how 'High in hand, his spear held against Irishmen, he pressed home his point'. This need not mean, however, that men like Thorfinn were embarked on a suicide mission. We know that the earl wore a golden helmet at Torfness, so no doubt he retained his body armour as well, while the shaft of a spear makes a useful parrying and blocking weapon and must to a large extent have substituted for the shield in the same way as a two-handed axe. And because it is no longer necessary to hold the shaft at the point of balance as it is when using it in one hand, the two-handed spear also has a greater potential reach, and so can keep an enemy at a distance where his own weapons cannot inflict damage.

It was well understood that the reach of the spear, and the fact that when used one-handed it did not require much space on either side to wield effectively, made it especially suitable for use in disciplined, close-order formations. The thirteenth-century Norwegian *Konungs Skuggsja* or 'King's Mirror' states that in these conditions a man armed with a spear is more effective than two with swords. By the time of the battles of Stirling Bridge in 1297, and Falkirk in the following year, the characteristic tactic of the Scottish armies was designed to take advantage of this fact: this was the 'schiltron' or 'schiltrum', basically a phalanx of infantry fighting shoulder to shoulder with long spears. So closely was this deployment associated with the Scots that Richard of Durham, writing of an English army at Boroughbridge in 1322, describes the spearmen as drawn up 'in schiltrom, after the Scottish fashion'. According to Walter Bower, William Wallace introduced a new system of organisation for his levies before Falkirk, with men grouped into units of five, ten and so on up to a thousand, but it is not clear whether this marks the origin of the schiltron tactics. Matthew Strickland has pointed out that Scottish armies employed long spears at the Standard in 1138, and that the Pictish Battle Stone at Aberlemno, as we have seen, shows a warrior using a long spear in both hands to ward off an enemy cavalryman. But it is striking that none of the battles discussed in our period – even Largs, which was fought only 34 years before Stirling Bridge – appears to have featured close-order infantry formations of the type adopted in the Wars of Independence. Instead the footsoldiers at Largs are described in *Haakon's Saga* as relying on a combination of spears, axes and missile weapons of various types, including bows and possibly slings. In fact Wallace's deployment at Falkirk in 1298, where the spearmen were used in a static defensive role with disastrous results, suggests that the schiltron of massed spears was then a recent development whose correct tactical employment was still being worked out.

One reason for the popularity of the spear in early mediaeval Scotland was the fact that the quantity of iron required for the blades of these weapons was relatively small. The country was not rich in good-quality iron ore, and in later centuries most sword blades and armour were imported from the Continent. The fourteenth-century chronicler Jean Froissart goes so far as to say that in his day even the iron for shoeing horses had to be bought in from Flanders

(Cannan, 2009). Swords, which need not only a greater quantity of metal, but also a high level of skilled craftsmanship, were therefore in short supply before the thirteenth century, carried only by the wealthiest warriors. But, as was the case in the rest of Britain and in Scandinavia, the increased availability of iron and gradually improving metalworking techniques eventually brought swords within the reach of most soldiers. Robert the Bruce's Statute of Arms of 1318 lists both sword and spear among the equipment that the poorer class of soldier should provide for himself. The great two-handed sword which was later associated with the Highlanders was probably a fifteenth-century innovation; the first illustrations of it come from the grave slabs of men killed at the Battle of Harlaw in 1411 (Melville, 2018). Smaller one-handed weapons are depicted on Sueno's stone and wielded by many of the Lewis chessmen, and it was these that were carried into battle in our period by those men able to afford them. There is no reason to suppose that the early development of the sword in Scotland followed a different path from elsewhere in Western Europe; the weapons of the Lewis chessmen seem to be of typical Viking style, double edged, slightly tapered and with lobated pommels, just as those depicted on the fourteenth or fifteenth-century gravestone of Bricius MacKinnon in Iona Abbey Museum, and the carving of an anonymous warrior in Kilmartin Church, Argyll, show fairly standard arming swords of that era. But during our period the most common hand-to-hand weapon after the spear was not the sword, but the axe.

Even in the late fourteenth century, when Froissart wrote of them, 'great axes, sharp and hard' were still a characteristic weapon of the Scots, whom he described as 'well expert' in their use. John Barbour, in his epic poem 'The Bruce', tells how Robert the Bruce's opponents at Dalrigh in 1306 fought on foot with axes, killing and wounding many of the royalists' horses. We cannot be certain how long axes had been in used in Scotland, but like the long spears, they are attested from pre-Viking Pictish times. The ninth-century Glamis Manse stone, for example, shows two men fighting with single-handed axes. The weapon was also, of course, closely associated with the Vikings, and it may have been under their influence that the long-handled two-handed versions appeared around the end of the tenth century. The long axes of the Irish were certainly derived from the weapons of the Norwegians; the *War of the Gaedhil with the Gaill*, describing the Battle of Clontarf in 1014, specifically calls them 'lochlann' (i.e. Norse) weapons. They are described in detail by Gerald de Barri, who visited Ireland in the 1180s and calls the carrying of axes an 'old and evil custom'. Gerald strongly disapproved of the way Irishmen habitually went armed with these weapons, because they lent themselves particularly well to treacherous assaults without warning. An axe, he says is 'always in the hand and ever ready', as it does not need to be unsheathed like a sword, or drawn like a bow, or even raised and pointed like a spear. According to Gerald the Irish axe was used one-handed despite the length of the haft, although illustrations in his *Topography of Ireland* show them being handled with two. But regardless of the technique used to wield it, we are told that neither mail armour nor helmets could protect against its blows. The Irish *Song of Dermot and the Earl* illustrates this with the story of Eoan Mear ('John the Mad'), the leader of the Orkney contingent at Dublin in 1171, who seems to have been a sort of latter-day berserker. He allegedly killed ten men with his axe, chopping off the leg of one mail-clad knight with a single blow. The axes at the Battle of Clontarf in 1014 were also described as especially useful for cutting through mail. Their effectiveness was due largely to the design of the head, which concentrates the force of a blow onto a smaller target area than the long blade of a sword. The shape of an axehead also lends itself to a variety of moves not available to a swordsman, such as catching the rim of an opponent's shield and pulling him off balance, or hooking his knee or ankle to bring him to the ground (Short, 2014). It is therefore by no means the poor relation of the sword as is often supposed, but a sophisticated weapon with its own repertoire of fighting techniques.

When used two-handed an axe, like a spear, can also be useful for parrying an enemy's attacks, and can even deliver blows with the butt of the shaft as well as with the blade. It is no doubt for this reason that a character in the Icelandic *Fostbreatha Saga* boasts that his axe will serve as a shield and a coat of mail as well as a weapon. By the thirteenth century the two-handed axe had begun to evolve towards a cut and thrust polearm like the later halberd. This is evident not only from the increased length of the shafts, but also from the appearance of axe heads with a sharp projection at the top which could be used to thrust like a spear. Several late mediaeval examples of this design have been found in Ireland, but there was an example in the Higgins Armory Museum (now closed) in Worcester, Massachusetts, which is dated as early as the twelfth century (Cannan, 2010). Eventually this type of weapon evolved into the Lochaber axe of the sixteenth century, which resembled a glaive or halberd, furnished with a point, a cutting edge and a hook for dismounting cavalry. The first written reference to this weapon appears to date from 1501, but John Major believed that what he calls a 'small halbert' was carried by 'the wild Scots of the north' by the time of Bannockburn in 1314, so it is just possible that a version of the Lochaber axe might have appeared as early as the Battle of Largs. Axes, at least the smaller one-handed versions, could even be thrown as well as swung in the hand. William of Newburgh describes an encounter, which must have taken place in around 1140, between Bishop Wimund of the Isles (see Chapter 5) and another unnamed bishop, who had refused Wimund's demand for tribute. As the opposing forces approached each other, this anonymous holy man decided to encourage his men by striking the first blow, so he threw a 'small axe', which struck the nearest of his opponents and brought him to the ground. Encouraged by this sign of God's favour his followers charged at once, killed many of their enemies, and forced Wimund himself to flee.

By the time that detailed accounts of Highland warfare begin to appear in the sixteenth century, the bow was well established as the principal missile weapon. Martin MacGregor (2012) suggests that archery came to prominence as an adjunct to the two-handed sword, with which it is often associated, and that the bow may have taken second place to the spear before the appearance of two-handed swords in the fifteenth century. However, we know that bows were carried by the Scots at Largs, and they are depicted in Pictish carvings made centuries before that. The Drosten Stone shows a kneeling archer carrying what is usually interpreted as a crossbow (Cannan, 2009). He is clearly depicted in a hunting context, about to take aim at a wild boar, but such weapons would also no doubt have played a role in warfare. In any case skill at archery is not easily developed from nothing, and the feats of archers like the MacRaes described in sixteenth-century accounts (Mackay, 1924) imply a long history of development. It seems likely that the bow did indeed gain in popularity in association with a two-handed close-combat weapon. From an ergonomic point of view this makes sense, as both needed two hands to wield and so worked best with the same sort of defensive equipment; it was desirable to have body armour that was as comprehensive as possible but allowed free movement of both arms, while a shield could be dispensed with as there was no free hand to hold it, thus saving on weight and improving mobility. The hand-to-hand weapon in question, however, would have been the two-handed Norse axe.

It is probable that mediaeval Highland archery owed a great deal to the Viking tradition, and it is noteworthy that while the Picts had evidently employed both conventional bows and crossbows, the Gaelic word for a bow, '*bogha*', is almost certainly derived from the Old Norse. The Vikings regarded skill at archery very highly, and many individual feats of arms with the bow are described in the Icelandic sagas. While they are no doubt exaggerated on occasion, one of the best known is recounted both by Snorri Sturlason in *Heimskringla* and by Gerald de Barri in his *Journey Through Wales*. This gives the story some sort of independent corroboration, even though Gerald's account is rather confused. According to Snorri, after his campaign in the Hebrides in 1098 King Magnus Barelegs sailed with a fleet from Orkney to attempt the conquest of North Wales, and was met on the shores of the Menai Strait by a Norman army led by two earls, named as 'Hugh the Proud and Hugh the Stocky'. The former was actually Hugh de Montgomery, the Earl of Shrewsbury, a prominent Norman baron. He was clad in a mail hauberk so complete that only his eyes were visible. This probably means that the mail flap sometimes seen in contemporary illustrations was drawn up over the lower part of his face, while his nose would have been protected by the nasal of his helmet. Gerald de Barri says that Hugh actually rode his horse into the sea in an act of bravado to confront the approaching longships. Magnus and an anonymous 'man from Halogaland' both took aim at him with their bows, and both arrows were loosed simultaneously. One struck Hugh's nose guard and bounced off, but the other hit him in the eye and went through his head, killing him. It can hardly have been possible to tell which arrow inflicted the fatal wound, but the man from Halogaland must have been diplomatic enough not to press his claim, because *Heimskringla* assures us that the king received the credit. We do not know the range at which this shot was made, though it can hardly have been very close if the Viking ships were not yet beached, but it was obviously remembered as an exceptional feat on the part of both men, made more difficult because it was achieved not from firm ground, but from a moving platform on the deck of a ship. The picking off of enemy leaders in this way is also a recurring theme in Scottish Highland warfare. For example, the fifteenth-century feud between the Mackay and Matheson clans was attributed to the action of Iver Matheson after the Battle of Drum na Coub in 1433; he arrived too late to take part in the fighting, but settled instead for stalking and killing the victorious Mackay chief, Angus Dubh, with an arrow (Matheson, 2014).

Fergus Cannan (2009) suggests that the Highland bow was 'less powerful' than the contemporary English longbow, on the grounds that it was shorter and drawn only to the chest, and also that the arrowheads in use were barbed designs intended for hunting, rather than the long, narrow bodkin points that would have been needed to pierce armour. None of these arguments seem very convincing. The first two appear to be based mainly on the famous illustration in the Carlisle Charter of 1316, which shows Scottish troops, including archers, attacking the defences of Carlisle. One of these archers does appear to be drawing a rather short bow to his chest, but this illustration is subject to all the usual caveats which apply to the literal interpretation of mediaeval art (Strickland & Hardy, 2005). The draw to the ear or jaw which we regard as typical of the so-called longbow is seldom shown in illustrations – no doubt for aesthetic reasons, because artists wished to avoid obscuring their subjects' faces – but was probably much more common in all times and places than illustrations would suggest, simply because it was such an obvious means of making the weapon more effective. Similar implausibly short bows and weak draws feature on the Bayeux Tapestry, for example. The character in the Carlisle Charter is clearly a minor player in the events depicted, and his lack of armour makes it unlikely that he represents a warrior of high rank. There is in any case no reason to suppose that he is a Highlander. And even if we concede that Scottish bows might have been on the short side, this does not prove that they lacked power. As Cannan himself admits, the Irish used short bows to considerable effect; a Catalan observer in Ireland in the late fourteenth century, Count John de Perilhos, remarked that the Irish bows were 'as short as half a bow of England, but they shoot as far as the English ones'. Cannan does not elaborate on his final remark that 'unless re-curved they cannot have offered much punch against armour', but the energy required to penetrate armour cannot be differentiated from that needed to propel the arrow a great distance, so a bow which can do one should equally well be able to do the other, unless it is shooting very light flight arrows, which we have no reason to suppose was the case here. Gaelic poetry makes it clear that good-quality Highland bows were made from yew (Mackay, 1924). This was generally acknowledged to be the best wood for the purpose and the one favoured by the English for their famed 'longbows'. As for the supposed ineffectiveness of barbed arrowheads, Hugh Soar (2010) cites modern experiments which show that, given a strong enough bow, it is not necessary to employ a specialised armour-piercing head to do serious damage to mail. It is true that plate armour would offer better resistance, but in the period under discussion here it was not yet in use, and the bare legs which were common among Highland warriors must have been especially vulnerable. An encounter at Eilean Donan Castle in around 1540 was known as the Battle of Arrow, because it was decided by a single shot which killed Donald Gorm MacDonald as his men were on the point of breaking into the castle (Mackay, 1924). In this case we are specifically told that the offending arrowhead was a barbed one, which struck Donald in the knee and caused fatal bleeding when it was pulled from the wound.

It is likely that the prominent role played by hunting in the Highlands influenced archery tactics in battle, especially among people like the Mackays of Sutherland, of whom Thomas Warren said in 1738 that they despised those who did not hunt the deer – no doubt because they recognised that the chase, like the cattle raid, was ideal training for war (Duffy, 2015). In fact skilled hunters could achieve the sort of fame normally reserved for victorious warriors. According to a tradition related by Alick George Mackay of Melness (quoted in Grannd, 2013) a piece of ground near Loch Hope known as Lon

Dhunnchaidh, or Duncan's Meadow, was so called after a famous poacher named Duncan, who killed a stag that no one else could approach. He achieved this by carrying a tree branch in front of him until he was close enough to shoot an arrow. (Unfortunately he was subsequently shot dead in his turn by Lord Mackay, who reasoned that so skilled a hunter must have been responsible for poaching his deer.) Although no contemporary source describes Highland archery tactics in detail, we can deduce that bowmen with this background would have fought as they hunted, in open order, dodging from one piece of cover to another and taking aim at individual targets, rather than loosing massed volleys on command from static positions like the English longbowmen. Such tactics would have been effective only at relatively close range, and it may have been as much for this reason as from a desire to close for hand-to-hand combat that Froissart tells us that 'in battle (the Scots) approach at once', and that they 'do not much trouble with the bow' once battle was joined. This, rather than any deficiencies in armament or individual skill, might explain why Scottish archers seldom achieved much in pitched battles against the English, despite the large numbers of bow-armed men which the Highland contingents must have been able to provide.

Armour and shields

Two radically different views of the defensive equipment of Scottish troops emerge from the sources quoted above. On the one hand we have the 'half naked' men at the Battle of the Standard, where Ailred of Rievaulx reports one of their leaders, Earl Malise of Strathearn, as arguing that mail hauberks were actually a burden rather than an asset, and that although he wore no armour he would advance further than any of the mail-clad knights in the army. In stark contrast is Gerald de Barri's description of the Islemen at Dublin as being 'completely clad in mail'. Obviously some men would have been able to afford better protection than others, but this was clearly not simply a case of making a virtue of necessity, as a high-ranking nobleman like Malise would surely have been able to purchase a mail hauberk if he had thought it worthwhile. One possibility is that the Norsemen had introduced or encouraged the wearing of armour in the far north and west, while an earlier tradition of lightly equipped skirmishers, perhaps derived from the Picts, still prevailed further south. Strathearn is in what is now Perthshire, and as we have seen, other unarmoured contingents at the Standard came from other southern districts such as Lothian and Galloway. Mail armour may even have fallen out of favour in some parts of Scotland under David I because of its association with the unpopular Norman newcomers favoured by the king. By the later Middle Ages, however, it had become the standard equipment of the gallowglasses and other Highland warriors, even as it began to be supplanted by plate elsewhere in Europe. This may have been, as MacGregor (2012) suggests, because mail was lighter than plate and more suitable for the aggressive, fast-moving fighting style favoured by its wearers, although hauberks which covered 'the whole body' as John Major describes, and in the words of George Buchanan extended 'even to their heels', can hardly have been convenient for such tactics. A knee-length reproduction of a Viking mail coat illustrated by Short (2014) weighed about 12kg (26lb), and a longer version as described by Buchanan must have weighed a quarter as much again. Body armour was often supplemented by an iron helmet, which seems to have been of fairly standard Western European type – either in Norman style with a nasal or, by the twelfth century, a kettle hat with a brim, as depicted on the Lewis chessmen.

In the sixteenth century the coat of mail ('*luireach*' in Gaelic) was invariably worn over a '*cotun*', a quilted jerkin stuffed with wool or cotton and covered with leather. How long this had been in use is not certain. Short (2014) has pointed out that there is no textual or archaeological evidence for such garments being worn in the Viking age, and the Gaelic term '*cotun*' is apparently derived, via the English aketon, from the Arabic '*al-qutun*', meaning cotton. It is therefore tempting to suppose that it was a late mediaeval innovation, perhaps imported by returning Crusaders. However, modern re-enactors are unanimous that some sort of padded garment is a necessity under mail, which otherwise gives no protection against a blow driving the metal rings into the wearer's flesh. We must therefore assume that the *cotun* was worn in our period, but being perishable it is unlikely to appear in archaeological excavations, and contemporary writers might have thought such a commonplace item unworthy of notice. One centrally placed infantryman on Sueno's Stone is wearing what at first sight appears to be a pleated kilt, but this would surely be anachronistic at such an early date, and the 'pleating' might instead be intended to represent quilted soft armour. As we have seen it is also possible that a leather coat of this sort is depicted on the Lewis chessmen. These examples hint at the possibility that the *cotun* might have been worn on its own by men unable or reluctant to wear mail, and that some of those disparaged as 'naked' might actually have been fairly well protected in this way, even if writers accustomed to the appearance of Norman-style knights might not have recognised their clothing as armour. This was certainly the case in the sixteenth century, when John Major says that the 'common folk... rush into battle having their whole body clad in a linen garment manifoldly sewed and painted or daubed with pitch, with a covering of deerskin.'

Shields seem to have progressed from small round bucklers, as depicted on some of the Pictish stones, to the much larger kite-shaped types carried by the Lewis chessmen, apparently identical to those used by twelfth-century cavalry and infantry throughout northern and western Europe. By the time of the Carlisle Charter in the early fourteenth century these 'kite shields' had been replaced by smaller 'heaters' of roughly similar shape (we do not know what terminology was used to describe them at the time; both these terms date from the nineteenth century). As with weaponry, it seems that Scotland was closely following European trends, and although the small round leather 'targe' associated with seventeenth and eighteenth-century Highlanders may have been in use earlier, we have no evidence of it from our period. Other shield types with more local distributions do occasionally appear in the sources, however. Some Pictish carvings show warriors carrying shields of rectangular shape, with or without projections at top and bottom in the shape of a capital letter H. These projections may simply be part of a wooden frame which was covered with leather, but it is possible that they were designed to catch an enemy's weapon, which suggests a very active, mobile style of fighting in contrast to the more solid formations of their Viking or English opponents. Until the eleventh century the Norsemen carried large, round wooden shields, usually painted red, and as noted above Gerald de Barri describes these as still in use in the 1170s. The story of the unfortunate Arni Hrafnsson, related in *Orkneyinga Saga*, also hints at the survival of these round shields. Arni was trying to seek sanctuary in a church in Kirkwall after a battle when his shield, which he had slung on his back by its carrying strap, became stuck in the doorway. As a kite shield would not normally have been much wider than a man's shoulders, we can assume that this one was of the old large, circular variety. In this context William Short (2014) remarks that a shield like this 'makes an excellent sail', catching any air movement and making it hard to control in high winds – something which might have been a serious problem in sea fights, as well as in windswept localities like Orkney and Caithness.

Tactics and the myth of the Highland warrior

Of the battles described below at least four: the second Battle of Skitten, Renfrew, Mam Garvia and Largs, were decided – one way or another – by a version of the headlong attack which became known in later centuries as the 'Highland charge'. This tactic has often been seen as a manifestation of an ancient 'Celtic' cultural approach to war which emphasised individual bravery and sought to overthrow the enemy at the first onset, demoralising him with a rapid and intimidating advance to contact, usually accompanied by war cries and discordant music. In this way the Celts would avoid protracted battles of attrition in which they would be at a disadvantage on account of their lack of discipline and defensive armour. This is attested as long ago as the Battle of Thermopylae in 279 BC, where the second-century Greek writer Pausanias describes how the Galatians 'rushed at their enemies like wild beasts, full of rage and temperament... even with arrows and javelins sticking through them they were carried on by sheer spirit while their life lasted' (quoted in Head, 1982). It has even been suggested that that this tradition persisted long enough to inspire the doomed charges at Culloden and Gettysburg (MacWhiney & Jamieson, 1982). David Stevenson (1994), however, argued in his study of the great seventeenth-century MacDonald commander Alasdair MacColla that the 'Highland charge' was not an ancient tradition at all, but had been invented in MacColla's own day as a counter to the superior firepower of musket-armed opponents. Both views have been contested, and as usual the truth probably lies somewhere in between the extremes. Certainly some Scottish troops favoured a rapid charge to contact long before the seventeenth century: at the Standard in 1138, for example, we have already seen how Ailred of Rievaulx says that the men from Galloway and Strathearn insisted on leading the attack despite their lack of armour. In the event they were shot down while trying to close with the English archers, pierced with arrows but slashing the air in 'blind madness' in a way that Pausanias would surely have recognised. The sixteenth-century historian John Major wrote of Highland battles of the previous century as lacking tactical direction and proceeding as a series of individual duels not very different from those described by Pausanias, so that 'every man made an end of his antagonist, or contrariwise'. More sophisticated tactics were, however, certainly in the Scots' repertoire from an early date – for example, the outflanking manoeuvre by a detached unit attempted at the third Battle of Skitten Moor (Chapter 2). And on other occasions, such as Torfness (Chapter 3), the impression gained from the admittedly brief sources is that the Scots allowed themselves to be attacked, either deliberately or because they were forestalled by a more aggressive opponent.

Writing of the later Middle Ages, Martin MacGregor (2012) considers that certain tactics were favoured over a long period by Scottish armies, and Highland ones in particular, but that these were governed not by cultural conservatism or an individualistic emphasis on man-to-man duels, but at least in part by environmental factors. Difficult terrain and a shortage of metals for defensive armour meant that mobility was always at a premium, while in forces numbering no more than a few thousand it was not feasible to allocate fighters to a large number of specialist roles. The Highland warrior, says MacGregor, was 'not defined by weapon or role, but multifunctional'. Everyone was expected to wield some sort of long-range missile to weaken the enemy as the opposing lines closed, then follow up in a charge to contact with a sword or similar hand-to-hand weapon. Without perpetuating a racial stereotype, it is nevertheless reasonable to acknowledge that the sort of pastoral lifestyle traditionally followed in the Highlands produced a population unusually adapted to war. In contrast to the situation in most of lowland Britain, the typical Highlander was not tied to a small plot of farmland for most of his life, but travelled widely over the hills with his cattle. Not only was he in the habit of moving his entire herd to summer pastures and back again in the autumn, but he always had to be alert to the perils which they might face from dangerous terrain, predators such as wolves, and of course human raiders. He was therefore accustomed to carry arms and negotiate rough country, and to use his own judgement when faced with unexpected situations. This was still the case at the time of the Jacobite Rebellions, when Highland units regularly outmarched regular troops and were much less dependent on the road network. Christopher Duffy (2015) quotes several eighteenth and early nineteenth-century writers on this subject: Alexander Home-Campbell, for example, described how the Highlanders 'do not walk like the generality of mankind, but trot and bounce like deer' from long practice in traversing the rough tracks through the mountains, while Ann Grant observed that 'civilised' people, accustomed to a life of routine, could never match 'the powers of those who must bend their minds every hour to come to some new and unpremeditated exertion'.

An emphasis on mobility and the necessity for bringing battles to a speedy conclusion also involved psychological warfare, an assault on the morale of the enemy by various methods with the aim of persuading him to break and run in the face of the initial charge. This may have been partly responsible for the shocking reputation of Scottish troops in the early Middle Ages, discussed by Matthew Strickland (1996), for refusing quarter to their enemies and collecting their severed heads as trophies. The theme of decapitation will be encountered in several of the following battle accounts, and on occasion even more gruesome mutilations might be inflicted in a conscious attempt to spread terror: in one conflict Somerled is said to have cut out the heart of the first man he killed, and then urged his followers to do the same. Another aspect of the psychological warfare associated with the Highland charge was the use of martial music, but the instruments of the early Middle Ages would not have been the bagpipes associated with the country today. Triple pipes, held directly in the mouth without a bag, are depicted on a number of Pictish stones, but bagpipes proper do not start to appear in art until the fourteenth century, and the earliest unequivocal reference to their use in battle comes from Jean de Beaugue, a French witness of the Battle of Pinkie in 1547 (West, 2012). Before the sixteenth century, according to George Buchanan, horns or trumpets had been the characteristic instrument of the Scots. Froissart describes these horns at Otterburn in 1388 as being 'some great, some small, and of all sorts, so that when they blow all at once, they make such a noise that it may be heard nigh four miles off.' The army of the bishop of Durham, he says, was 'sore abashed' by this noise, imagining that 'all the devils in hell had been among them'. That the tradition was a very ancient one is suggested by the nineteenth-century discovery at Deskford in Banffshire of a bronze carnyx from the later Iron Age, which is now in the National Museum of Scotland. The carnyx was an elongated trumpet topped with a stylised animal head, which according to classical sources was blown in battle by Celtic armies throughout Europe. Diodorus Siculus describes its 'harsh sound which suits the tumult of war', a description confirmed by modern reconstructions. We can therefore deduce that the Scottish forces engaged in the battles described here would have advanced to the accompaniment of a similar cacophony of sound. By the sixteenth century each Highland clan also had its distinctive 'slogan' or war cry, and there are hints in the sources that this was also the case in our period: the Galwegians at the Standard, for example, advanced accompanied by shouts of 'Albani!', presumably referring to Alba, the then current name for the kingdom of Scotland.

Ships and castles

Ships and boats of various kinds feature in several of our battles, as might be expected in a region with a long indented coastline and numerous islands, where communication by sea was often far easier than by land. In earlier times the typical Scottish boat was the skin-covered curragh, which was buoyant and easily handled, but the method of construction could not be scaled up to produce vessels able to transport large numbers of men or to provide a stable platform for fighting. Not long after the first contact with the Viking raiders, therefore, wooden ships of Scandinavian type seem to have quickly replaced the old curraghs, at least for military purposes. These were of what is known as 'clinker' construction, with a hull made of overlapping planks joined together with iron rivets. Such vessels were stronger and more seaworthy than those covered with hides or relying on the alternative 'carvel' method of wooden construction, with the planks simply butted together and fixed to a frame. The Scandinavian types are often referred to generally as 'longships', but strictly this term applies only to the larger vessels of relatively narrow beam, built for speed under oars rather than seaworthiness or cargo capacity, and so optimised for war rather than trade. Evidence from Scotland is confined mainly to representations carved on memorial stones of the later Middle Ages, but a number of ships have been excavated from sites in Scandinavia which can give us an idea of the variety of designs in use in the Viking age (Williams, 2014). Some of these vessels appear to have been buried deliberately as part of the funeral rites of important men, while others were sunk either by accident or as blockships for the defence of harbours. In the 1950s and 60s six such blockships were found at Skuldelev in Roskilde Fjord in Denmark, where they had been placed in the eleventh century to form a blockade outside the port of Roskilde. One of these, known as Skuldelev 5, is of typical long and narrow longship proportions, but is much smaller than the great vessels which we hear of in the sagas. As reconstructed it is 17.3 metres long and has room for about twenty-six rowers; like most Viking ships it was designed to be propelled by either sail or oars depending on circumstances. It is partly built of oak from western Norway, which was cut around 1030, but some sections are of ash and pine instead, and show signs of having been recycled from older ships; for example some of the oar ports seem to have been designed for a larger vessel, and have been covered over and new ones cut in their place. Furthermore, the ship had seen some hard use and had been repeatedly repaired by the time it was sunk. Skuldelev 5 probably represents the sort of vessel which would be provided by poorer localities for the leidang, as well as those employed by small private expeditions. The 'small and poorly manned' ships from the Hebrides which are recorded as taking part in the Tankerness campaign of 1136 (Chapter 4) might well have been very similar.

The vessels which were used in the Isles between the twelfth and sixteenth century are often referred to in English as 'galleys', but they were very different from the usual Mediterranean-type galley that the word brings to mind. They were in fact modified longships, which differed mainly in their smaller size and in the use of a rear-mounted rudder. This innovation was apparently introduced around the time of Somerled to replace the old-fashioned side-mounted steering oar, but the theory that Somerled invented it can be discounted: it was already well known elsewhere in Europe, and is in fact better suited to larger ships than to the small Hebridean galleys (Rixson, 1998). These galleys were known at the time as '*lymphads*' or '*birlinns*'. '*Lymphad*' is an Anglicisation of the Gaelic '*long fada*', which literally means 'long ship', and its line of descent from its Viking progenitor is obvious from its design. The term was generally used for the largest type of Hebridean galley, which was designed, like Skuldelev 5, for between twenty and twenty-six rowers. A *birlinn* was similar in design but usually somewhat smaller, perhaps employing around sixteen or twenty oars. Denis Rixson argues that the boats used on the west coast of Scotland and in the Hebrides became smaller over time as the importance of international seaborne trade declined, but they may always have been smaller than their equivalents in the north. The tenth-century ship discovered in 2011 at Port an Eilean Mhoir on the Ardnamurchan Peninsula was buried with an individual who, from the weapons and other goods found, was apparently of high rank, but the vessel itself is only five metres long (archaeologyscotland.org.uk).

In the later Middle Ages strategy in the Isles was dominated by a combination of ships and stone castles. According to Martin MacGregor (2012) 'There was no point in a naval strategy without a castle strategy... Castle keepership and naval command went together.' However there is little evidence for dependence on stone fortifications in the period covered by this book. The northern and western isles are still studded with the remains of the round stone towers or 'brochs' unique to this part of Scotland, which were erected in Iron Age and early Pictish times, but by the time the Vikings arrived they were no longer being built, although they were sometimes occupied for defence in emergencies. For example, *Orkneyinga Saga* tells of how in 1153 Earl Harald Maddadsson unsuccessfully besieged the broch on Mousa in Shetland where his mother was being held captive, and local tradition claims that the edifice at Dun Carloway on Lewis was still in use during the clan battles of the sixteenth century. But castles of the type introduced into England by the Normans in 1066 remained very rare in northern Scotland. Some of the earliest, the structures erected by William the Lion at Ederdour, Dunskeath and Auldearn in Ross and Moray (see Chapter 6), were probably built of earth and timber rather than stone. The latter material probably first came back into favour in Orkney, where timber was not available, but even there no remains pre-date the structure known as Cubby Roo's Castle on the island of Wyre, which *Orkneyinga Saga* says was built by Kolbein Hruga in around 1145. It has been suggested (for example on the Historic Environment Scotland website) that the square tower at Old Wick in Caithness was built by Earl Harald Maddadsson of Orkney not long after this, perhaps in the 1150s, but this remains unproven by archaeology. The oldest stone castle on the west coast is generally thought be Castle Sween in Knapdale, Argyll, which dates from around 1200 (MacGregor, 2012). It is therefore safest to assume that most of the protagonists in the battles discussed in this book, except perhaps for the later kings of Scots and earls of Orkney, did not enjoy the advantages of the kind of fortified bases that were commonplace in the rest of Western Europe.

Chapter 2

The Killing Field of Skitten Moor

Dates: *c*.892, *c*.980, *c*.1000 AD

Location: Skitten Moor, near Wick, Caithness

Combatants: Earl Sigurd the Mighty of Orkney versus Maelbrigte, Mormaer of Moray

Earl Ljot of Orkney versus MacBeth, Mormaer of Moray

Earl Sigurd the Stout of Orkney versus Finnleik, Mormaer of Moray

Outcome: three Orkney victories

A t some time during the late eighth or early ninth century AD, the far north-east of what is now Scotland, once a stronghold of Celtic culture, became a new frontier zone. Modern archaeological discoveries have shown that the Orkney Isles had supported a thriving civilisation as long ago as the Neolithic Age; the Standing Stones of Stenness, for example, are thought to be the oldest such site in Britain, and may have inspired – even if only indirectly – the builders of Stonehenge. Later, in the Iron Age, the islands were studded with the stone towers which we know as 'brochs'. The question of whether these were originally defensive structures remains controversial, but their presence certainly attests to a relatively numerous population, and one which was well enough organised to undertake ambitious building work. These people are usually considered to be closely related to the contemporary inhabitants of the Scottish mainland, and are known by the same name, 'Picts'. By the late sixth century, when Saint Columba brought Christianity to the north, most of Scotland was apparently controlled by two Pictish kingdoms, one based in the south in the fertile country along the Tay and Forth rivers, and the other, Fortrin, centred on the Inverness region at the mouth of the Moray Firth. We do not know whether the Orkney Isles were ever actually ruled from Inverness, but they were clearly subject to many of the same influences, and were converted to Christianity towards the end of the sixth century by missionaries sent by Columba. Two hundred and fifty years later, however, both the new religion and, apparently, the Picts themselves, had vanished from the islands. Their place names were now Norwegian; their gods Thor and Odin; their inhabitants, to all appearances, Vikings.

The coming of the Vikings

The causes of the Norse incursions into western Europe were complex, and much debate continues about the relative influence of factors like the introduction of more seaworthy ship designs, overpopulation in Scandinavia, and the consolidation of royal authority with the consequent flight of rivals to seek their fortune overseas. From the point of view of the people of the British Isles, however, these incursions were completely unexpected. Under the year 793 the *Anglo-Saxon Chronicle* described how 'the raiding of heathen men miserably devastated God's church in Lindisfarne island'. Even such a well-travelled and well-informed scholar as Alcuin of York commented in a famous letter that:

> Never before in Britain has such a terror appeared as this we have now suffered at the hands of the heathen. Nor was it thought possible that such an inroad from the sea could be made.

But, although there is no documentary evidence from the north, it seems likely that by the 790s the people of Shetland and Orkney were already all too familiar with raiders of this type. Their islands were, after all, obvious staging posts on the sea route from Norway to Britain, and Orkney also offered fertile land which was well suited to the farming methods of Norse settlers. Archaeological discoveries at Pool and Scar on the island of Sanday may provide evidence for settlement as early as the late eighth century (Batey & Sheehan, in Fitzhugh & Ward, eds, 2000). Certainly by the 870s at the latest both Orkney and Shetland were firmly under Scandinavian occupation, and the Pictish population had disappeared from the record so completely that many writers have assumed that it had been entirely replaced. However, there is no conclusive evidence to determine whether this dramatic change occurred violently, by mass murder or an early form of 'ethnic cleansing', or whether it happened more gradually and more peacefully.

In fact the question of the fate of the Picts has been debated, often furiously, since the 1970s. At that time the excavation at Buckquoy in Orkney of what appeared to be Viking houses full of Pictish artefacts led Anna Ritchie (1977) to propose a scenario of peaceful integration. Since then arguments and counter-arguments have been drawn from various disciplines. It has been suggested that the *Life* of the ninth-century St Findan describes a Christian bishop still living in Orkney (C.J. Omand, in Berry and Firth, 1986), but although the text relates Findan's miraculous escape from Viking captivity on one of the islands, it goes into few details about the residence of the bishop with whom he found refuge except that it contained an extensive range of high hills, not a feature associated with Orkney. Some archaeologists have questioned whether the buildings at Buckquoy are really of Viking date, while others have pointed to the absence of mass graves which might be evidence for genocide. Place names in Orkney and Shetland are overwhelmingly Scandinavian, but a similar preponderance of Anglo-Saxon names in eastern England is not usually taken nowadays as conclusive proof of total population replacement (see for example the discussion in my *Offa and the Mercian Wars*, Pen & Sword, 2012).

The most detailed genetic study to date confirms that the present population of the northern isles stands out as distinct from the rest of Britain because of the degree of Norse genetic admixture, but nevertheless estimates this at only around 18% in Orkney and Shetland, compared to 7% in the Hebrides (Gilbert et al, 2019).

From some points of view, therefore, it may be misleading to consider the people of Orkney from the ninth century onwards as being purely 'Norsemen' or 'Vikings', but that is how they are characterised in the main surviving source for the period, *Orkneyinga Saga*. The characters mentioned in the saga as living on the islands all have unequivocal Scandinavian names, so the indigenous inhabitants who must still have been present either adopted the language and culture of the newcomers very quickly, or were of such low status that they could be ignored. The twelfth-century *Historia Norwegie* does mention that the islands had previously been occupied not only by the Picts, but also by 'papar', Christian monks and hermits who no doubt valued the solitude of the outlying islands, but then they too disappear from this narrative. Culturally and politically, then, Scandinavians were now dominant, but although the first waves of immigrants may have appropriated the land by force, they did not represent a royal army of conquest sent from Norway. Scandinavian settlement patterns in northern Scotland were always very different from those in England and Ireland. In the latter countries they were largely centred around trading centres like York and Dublin, where substantial armies could be raised and equipped, but in northern Scotland towns were fewer and smaller, and the great majority of incomers seem to have settled in rural areas and lived by farming, supplemented by small-scale seaborne plundering expeditions led by local warlords. In fact, according to *Orkneyinga Saga*, many of those based in Orkney and Shetland were freelance pirates who were launching damaging raids not only against the Hebrides and further south, but also against Norway itself. Eventually, in 874, the Norwegian king Harald

Harfagri, or 'Fairhair', was provoked into taking action against these raiders, sailing west to claim Orkney as part of his dominions and appointing Rognvald Eysteinsson, lord of the coastal region of More, as its earl with the mission of pacifying it. It is likely that by this time Caithness, in the north-east of the Scottish mainland, had also begun to receive the first Norse immigrants, probably from Orkney rather than directly from Scandinavia. On a modern map Norse place names are universal in the relatively flat and fertile region lying north and east of the Thurso and Wick rivers, while in the hillier country further south and west Gaelic names begin to predominate. Barbara Crawford (2013) has reviewed the archaeological and place-name evidence for this settlement and considers that it dates from not long before the year 900. On the assumption that farmers could only put down roots once some sort of political authority was in place to defend them, she suggests that the large-scale settlement of Caithness probably followed the conquests of Rognvald's brother and successor, Sigurd Eysteinsson 'the Mighty', who ruled from around 880 until 892.

Sigurd the Mighty

Orkneyinga Saga tells us that at some point Rognvald had transferred his authority over his earldom voluntarily to his brother Sigurd, who at first ruled in alliance with another famous Viking, Thorstein the Red. Sigurd is credited with the conquest not only of Caithness, but also of extensive territories on the Scottish mainland in Moray, Ross and even Argyll. It was from these conquests that the earl earned his nickname of '*hinn riki*', or as it is usually translated, 'the Mighty'. In fact place-name evidence suggests that the Scandinavians never settled as far south as Moray in any numbers, but there is a cluster of Norse names in Ross, which Barbara Crawford suggests may be derived from people who arrived there during one of the brief periods of Norse hegemony in the region. The strategic importance of the valley of the River Oykel and the coastal districts of Easter Ross as sources of timber for shipbuilding has been discussed in the introduction, but this river, and especially the wide lower section known as the Kyle of Sutherland, would also have been a natural frontier between the Norse-occupied country to the north and the native rulers who still flourished around Inverness and along the Moray Firth.

Not surprisingly this frontier became an active war zone, and it was in Sigurd's day that the first of a series of arranged battles took place in Caithness between the earls of Orkney and their Scottish counterparts. This must have taken place around the year 892, which is the generally accepted date of Sigurd's death. According to *Orkneyinga Saga* a certain Maelbrigte, who is described as 'Earl of the Scots', agreed to meet Sigurd with forty mounted men each in order to settle a dispute between them. We are not told what this dispute was about, but if Sigurd was responsible for encouraging settlers from Orkney to migrate to the mainland, the existing inhabitants of Caithness might have appealed to a local magnate for protection. Neither is it clear exactly who this Maelbrigte was, because very little is known about the political situation in Scotland at this period. In fact, to refer to 'Scotland' at all may still be an anachronism. The reigning monarch at the time, Donald II (Domnall mac Causantin), who occupied the throne from around 889 to 900, is thought to have been the first of his line to have been referred to by contemporaries – using the Gaelic word for the kingdom – as 'King of Alba' (Foster, 2014). Previously Kenneth MacAlpin and his successors had been described (for example by the *Chronicle of the Kings of Alba*) as ruling two separate polities, Dal Riata and Pictavia or Pictland, and some scholars do not consider that the new kingdom was fully consolidated until the reign of Donald's successor Constantine II (Causantin mac Aeda). So it is quite likely that Maelbrigte was a member of the old

Pictish aristocracy, probably a forebear of the later 'mormaers' of Moray.

The name Moray, or Muireb, then denoted a territory far larger than the modern district, incorporating not only the southern shore of the Moray Firth east of Inverness, but also the entire valley of the River Spey as far south as the Pass of Drumochter, which marks the watershed between the Spey, flowing north, and the tributaries of the Tay. It may have been the successor of the ancient Pictish kingdom of Fortriu, which had been destroyed by the Vikings in the early ninth century. In the north Moray was apparently bounded only by the Norse lands in Sutherland and Caithness, and so must have extended as far as the River Oykel. Unfortunately we can be less certain about Moray's political status. From the tenth century onwards it was controlled by men bearing the title of 'mormaer', which has been derived from Gaelic terms meaning either 'Great Steward' or 'Sea Steward'. Sally Foster (2014) argues that, although the word itself is not attested from before the early tenth century, the office may have had its origins in Pictish times, and been incorporated by Kenneth MacAlpin or his descendants into the structure of their kingdom. Later in the Middle Ages the territories held by the mormaers became conventional feudal earldoms, but it is likely that in Maelbrigte's day they enjoyed much greater autonomy. The Irish *Annals* persist in calling the rulers of Moray 'kings', and as we shall see it was not unusual for them to mount military challenges to the kings of Scots as late as the twelfth century. It was not until after the Battle of Stracathro in 1130 that the Scottish rulers succeeded in planting their own vassals in Moray and reducing it to subservience. The Norse sagas often seem to confuse the mormaers of Moray with the rulers of Scotland, and this may reflect genuine uncertainty on all sides about how much autonomy they actually had. So although they probably acknowledged some sort of tributary relationship to the Scottish kings, in their conflicts with the Norsemen in Orkney and Caithness they seem to have acted as independent powers. Maelbrigte's name is a common one and we will encounter it again, but it is significant that it is apparently derived from the Irish or Gaelic tongue, in which it means 'servant of Saint Brigid'. By this time Moray, once a Pictish stronghold, seems to have become largely Gaelic-speaking. This was a result of the growing influence of the Scots from the old kingdom of Dal Riata, whose name was around this time beginning to be applied to the whole of 'Scotland'.

The location of the meeting between Sigurd and Maelbrigte is not specified in the sketchy account in the saga, but the site must have lain somewhere near the coastal road which led into Caithness from the south, along the northern shore of the Moray Firth. It might have been somewhere along the Oykel, or alternatively it could have been in the vicinity of Skitten Moor, further north, which as we shall see was a favoured spot for such meetings on subsequent occasions. The location of any encounter between the lords of Moray and those of Caithness must have been largely determined by the local geography, which allowed any invader a very limited choice of routes. A glance at a map might give the impression that the border between Caithness and the rest of Scotland is too long to be easily defensible, but the interior of the country is very different from the rolling grasslands of coastal Caithness, which still evoke the sort of landscape that must have attracted the Norse farmers to the mainland. Today central Sutherland and the inland parts of Caithness constitute one of the most sparsely populated places in Europe, if not in the world – Sutherland as a whole has a population density similar to that of Namibia – where even at the height of the holiday season it is possible to drive for hours along the narrow roads and meet no one. Much of the terrain is dominated by the 'Flow Country', an immense expanse of peat bog studded with small lochs and pools, which is more reminiscent of the Arctic tundra than of anything else in the British landscape. For most of the year it is exposed to bitterly cold winds, while in the summer, if the wind is not blowing, the onslaught of clouds of biting midges can be almost unbearable. Even today, when it has been partly drained for forestry, large tracts of it are almost impassable. On the other hand, those visitors who do travel here are quickly made aware of the tragic story of the Highland Clearances, which allegedly created this great solitude in the early nineteenth century by sweeping away whole communities in order to clear the land for sheep. We know from both written sources and archaeological remains that some districts, such as Strath Naver in Sutherland, were indeed once thriving farming districts far more densely peopled than they are today.

Thus we are presented with two contrasting views: of 'Britain's last great wilderness' on the one hand, and on the other the homeland of a great diaspora, now scattered across America and other far-flung parts of the globe. The situation in the early Middle Ages, one suspects, was somewhere between the two extremes, with human settlement more extensive in some favoured spots than it is today, but with overall numbers kept low by a combination of the inhospitable land and the endemic violence of a region far from the reach of laws and governments. The description in *Orkneyinga Saga* of the killing of the formidable matriarch Frakokk by Svein Asleifsson in the twelfth century has her assailants travelling 'by forest and mountain above all the settlements', before descending unexpectedly on Frakokk's homestead in the Strath of Kildonan. This tells us that the region was sparsely populated enough that a war party of around eighty men could travel undetected into the middle of it by keeping to the woods and hills. There were apparently routes overland to the north and west coasts via the straths of Kildonan and Naver; the name of the now-abandoned village of Rosal in upper Strath Naver derives from the Norse for 'horse field', which suggests that it was known as a spot where travellers could stop to rest and graze their horses (Crawford, 2013). But all these routes involved a long detour, and it would probably have been very difficult to supply a mediaeval army.

A small mounted force of the type which Maelbrigte led could no doubt have got through, but it was actively seeking the enemy on this occasion, and so there would have been no advantage in disappearing into the interior.

We can therefore be fairly sure that the first documented clash between Viking and Scot took place somewhere near the North Sea coast in Sutherland or Caithness, with the opposing contingents riding onto the field at a prearranged time with their retinues. Naturally, things did not go according to plan. Sigurd turned up not with forty men, but with eighty, two on each horse, having decided, as the saga reports without apparent irony, 'that the Scots weren't to be trusted'. Maelbrigte, who had in fact stuck to the agreement, spotted the trick from a distance and decided to fight anyway, although with his horses less heavily burdened he could have easily escaped to safety. Instead he urged his forty followers to make an immediate charge with the aim of killing at least one of the Norsemen each before they fell, but Sigurd was prepared for this. He dismounted half his men and sent them to make a flank attack, while the remaining forty charged the Scots on horseback. The outcome was that Maelbrigte and all his men were killed, and the victorious Orkney men rode home with the Scotsmen's heads tied to their saddles as trophies. The story is well known of how Maelbrigte obtained his posthumous revenge, as Sigurd received a scratch on the leg from his victim's protruding tooth and died of the infected wound. The earl was buried in a mound on the shores of the River Oykel, probably in the vicinity of a farm named Cyder Hall on the north bank near Dornoch, the name of which is derived from an earlier 'Sigurdarhaugr' or 'Sigurd's mound' (Crawford, 2013).

Sigurd's successors

Sigurd the Mighty was succeeded by his son Guthorm, who died childless after a reign of only a year. Rognvald of More, who obviously still considered himself to have a role in the government of Orkney, despite his earlier abdication in favour of Sigurd, sent his own son Hallad to take charge, but he turned out not to be equal to the task of protecting the people from unruly Vikings and resigned his position and returned to Norway. Rognvald then despatched his youngest son, Einar; according to the saga Einar was regarded until then as a failure and was sent west mainly to get rid of him, but Rognvald provided him with a ship and the Norwegian king, Harald, appointed him to the earldom. The new earl – nicknamed 'Turf Einar' because he was the first Norseman to adopt the Scottish habit of digging peat for fuel – quickly confounded the doubters, and proved to be one of Orkney's most effective rulers. First he brought the two most troublesome of the Viking raiders to battle and killed them both. Soon after this King Harald's son Halfdan attempted to stage a coup in Norway. He murdered Rognvald and tried to usurp his authority, but was forced to flee from his father's wrath and ended up in Orkney. His arrival terrified the people, and many of them either surrendered to him or fled, but Einar gathered an army on the mainland, then returned and engaged Halfdan in a battle at sea. The invaders were defeated, and in the failing light of evening Halfdan fell overboard. Einar's men fished him out the following day – whether alive or dead is not stated – and Einar made a gruesome example of him, cutting his ribs away from his spine, pulling out his lungs and spreading them on his back in a ritual dedication to Odin. This 'blood eagle' is sometimes regarded as a sensationalist invention of the saga writers, but the verses quoted on this occasion, in which Einar boasted of his butchering of the king's son, have the ring of truth.

King Harald's view of this affair was obviously ambivalent, since Halfdan was his son but also a rebel and a fugitive from justice. The king therefore refused to allow Halfdan's brothers to take their own bloody revenge, but instead sailed in person to Orkney and imposed a fine of sixty gold marks on the community. Instead of paying this by means of a tax on his subjects, as would have been the normal practice, Einar agreed to pay it out of his own funds (probably the proceeds of plundering expeditions in Scotland and elsewhere) in return for what amounted to a mortgage on the lands of the farmers, who it appears had previously owned them outright. Einar died peacefully around the year 910, after a long and successful reign, and was succeeded by his son Thorfinn 'Skull Splitter' after his two other sons, Arnkel and Erlend, were killed fighting in England under King Eirik 'Blood Axe'. Thorfinn, another strong ruler, lived until 963, but after his death the rivalry among his five sons again threatened to set the Norsemen against each other. *Orkneyinga Saga* puts the blame on Ragnhild, wife of the eldest son Arnfinn, who first schemed with the second of the brothers, Havard, to murder her husband, then incited their nephew Einar to kill Havard. Eventually she married the fourth brother, Ljot, who succeeded to the earldom. However the youngest of Thorfinn's sons, Skuli, fled to Scotland where he persuaded the king – who at this date was presumably the little known Duff (Dub mac Mail Choluim) – to grant him the title of earl. This early intervention in northern affairs was an ominous portent of things to come, but at this date the kings of Scots were still in no position to impose their authority north of the Kyle of Sutherland. It seems likely, however, that the earls of Orkney had lost control of their lands in Ross and Moray during the disturbed decades following the death of Sigurd the Mighty, leaving their holdings on the Scottish mainland restricted once more to the north-eastern portion of Caithness.

We are told that Skuli mustered troops in Caithness, presumably in the southern and western districts which were beyond Ljot's control, after which he invaded Orkney. There he was defeated by Ljot and forced to flee south again, while Ljot remained in Caithness and raised his own army there. When Skuli returned it was with what the saga describes as an army 'supplied by the King of Scots and Earl MacBeth'. This MacBeth was possibly an ancestor of the eleventh-century Scottish king of the same name, but nothing else is known about him, though the saga writer's use of the term 'earl' implies that he was considered to be of similar social standing to the earls of Orkney. Like Maelbrigte before him, he may have held the rank of mormaer of Moray. A battle was fought between Ljot on the one hand, and MacBeth and Skuli on the other, in 'the Dales of Caithness', again probably somewhere on the road along the east coast. All we know of the fighting is that the Scots at first attacked fiercely, but failed to make an impression on the steadfast defenders. The Vikings were probably deployed in their usual fashion in a line several ranks deep, an arrangement which not only allowed for the rapid replacement of casualties in the front rank, but would also make it harder for a skilled opponent to break through the line by killing the man in front of him and then threaten the warriors still fighting on either side of the gap from the flank or rear. Ljot distinguished himself not only in combat, but also by continually encouraging his men and exhorting them to stand fast. Eventually the Scottish army disintegrated, and Skuli was killed in a rearguard action. MacBeth, however, was reluctant to accept Ljot's control of Caithness, and sometime around the year 980 he travelled north again with a large army. The saga does not say whether the ensuing battle was another arranged encounter like that between Sigurd and Maelbrigte, but this time the location is specifically named as Skitten in Caithness.

The area usually identified today as Skitten Moor lies inland from Sinclair's Bay, just north of the town of Wick. The name does not appear on the modern Ordnance Survey map, but James Gray (1922) identified it as Skida Myre 'in Watten', while James Miller (2012) calls it 'a bare stretch of high ground a few miles inland from Wick'. Watten is a small village at the eastern end of Loch Watten, about six miles inland from Wick, so the two versions need not necessarily be incompatible. The whole area is in fact quite flat and featureless, and it is impossible to be more precise about the exact location of the battlefield than to say that it must have been somewhere between Sinclair's Bay, north of Wick, and Loch Watten. We do not know whether MacBeth came all the way from Moray by land, or whether he transported his army to Caithness by sea, or indeed whether he possessed a fleet capable of such a task; but either route would have led him to somewhere in this vicinity. Much of the Caithness coast is rocky and fringed with cliffs, but Sinclair's Bay has a long sandy beach where ships could have been brought ashore in relative safety. Alternatively, the most likely land route north would also have passed, as the A99 still does, close to the coast, between Sinclair's Bay and the Loch of Wester, and this would have been a logical place to intercept an enemy coming from the direction of Moray. The coast south of Wick might have been less suitable for a pitched battle as it seems to have been more wooded than it is today – or was before the twentieth-century vogue for forestry plantations. For example, James Harting (1880) quotes a tradition that the woods on the hills of Yarrow were cut down around 1500 in order to destroy a lair of wolves. It seems that for a combination of these reasons Skitten Moor, wherever its precise location might have been, was by this time recognised as a logical place to block an invader's advance from the south. This Ljot duly did. The Orkney army was outnumbered, but the saga writer says that the battle was nevertheless brief, with the Scots being forced back and then dissolving into flight. However the clash must have been fierce while it lasted, because many men were wounded on both sides. Among them was Earl Ljot, who returned to Orkney but later died of his injuries. According to local tradition a standing stone at Bower, south of Castletown on the north coast of Caithness, was erected as his memorial, but in fact the stone is probably much older than the tenth century. Ljot was succeeded by his brother Hlodvir, Thorfinn Skull Splitter's third son, of whom the saga says simply that he 'ruled well' and 'died in his bed' around the year 991, after which his son Sigurd became earl.

Sigurd the Stout

The last of the encounters on or near Skitten Moor took place in the reign of Sigurd Hlodvirsson, who was distinguished from his illustrious predecessor Sigurd I 'the Mighty' by the nickname of 'Digri', usually translated as 'the Stout'. In fact, as Dr Crawford points out, the Norse term implies steadfastness and power rather than obesity, and the Latin *Genealogy of the Earls* describes him not only as '*corpolentus*' ('corpulent'), but also '*robustus… magnus et strenuissimus*', words which can be rendered as 'robust, great and valiant'. He was remembered, therefore, for his commanding presence and his ability as a warrior. *Njal's Saga* credits him with ruling Sutherland, Ross and Moray as well as Orkney and Caithness, and *Orkneyinga Saga*, by implication contrasting him with his immediate predecessors, says that he was strong enough to defend Caithness against the Scots as well as going plundering every summer as far afield as Ireland. The key event in this connection was a confrontation with another 'Scottish earl', named in the saga as Finnleik, who one summer issued a challenge for Sigurd to fight him at Skitten. It was this Battle of Skitten Moor that saw the debut of one of the most iconic symbols of the Viking way of war – the magical raven banner of Earl Sigurd. The saga writer tells us that when Sigurd received the challenge he was worried, because he believed that his enemies outnumbered him by at least seven to one. So he first secured the allegiance of the Orkney farmers by restoring the ancient land rights which they had lost under 'Turf Einar', then went to consult his mother, an Irish princess named Eithne, who had a reputation as a sorceress. She made for him a richly embroidered banner which bore the image of a raven, so cleverly designed that when the fabric flapped in the wind the bird appeared to be flying. She told Sigurd that she believed it would bring victory to the army that followed it, but death to the man who carried it.

Some corroboration for the saga's story comes from another of the great Icelandic literary works, *Njal's Saga*. This deals mainly with events in Iceland, but the sea routes between Iceland and Scotland were well travelled by this time, and the story's main characters were involved in Scottish and Irish affairs on several occasions. The saga writer tells the story of how Njal's sons, Grim and Helgi, first encountered a character who was to become central to Njal's story, Kari Solmundarsson. This must have happened some time during the reign of Sigurd the Stout in Orkney, but exactly when is unclear. Later in the story the king of Scots is referred to as 'Melkolf', which might be a version of Mael Coluim or Malcolm, in which case it could be dated to the reign of Malcolm II, between 1005 and 1034, but the Norse sagas are often unreliable about events in Scotland. *Orkneyinga Saga* places what are presumed to be the same events before Earl Sigurd's conversion to Christianity by Olaf Tryggvasson, and so by implication before Olaf's death, which is known to have taken place in the year 1000.

Grim and Helgi had been allowed by their father to travel abroad, and had taken passage on a ship belonging to Bard the Black and Olaf, son of Ketil of Elda. Exactly what the purpose of the voyage was is not explained, but although most of the crew are described as merchants, Njal clearly expected his sons to meet with trouble, so they were probably planning to combine trading with more violent methods of acquiring wealth as the opportunity offered. They were driven south from Iceland by strong north winds, and then became lost in a dense fog, so that when they finally approached land none of them had any idea where they might be. They entered what the saga describes as a fjord, with land on both sides and heavy surf on the shores, so they anchored for the night at a safe distance from the coast. There are some clues in the saga account which suggest a probable location for this fjord. It was clearly a sea loch or inlet of the sea, narrow enough for land to be visible on both sides, but large and deep enough for sizeable fleets to manoeuvre. As Kari's ships later approached from the south en route from the Hebrides to Orkney, we can deduce that it was somewhere on the west coast of Scotland. We are also told that there was a group of islands within the loch, in the lee of which vessels could shelter. There are several possible candidates, but the largest of them, and the most likely, is Loch Broom in Wester Ross. Today the ferry from the mainland port of Ullapool to Stornoway on the Isle of Lewis takes this route, passing close to the Summer Isles at the mouth of the loch.

By morning the wind had dropped and the sea was calmer, but before the merchants could raise their anchor they saw thirteen ships coming out from the shore to intercept them. A parley ensued, during which they learned that the leaders of the local fleet were Grjotgard and Snaekolf, sons of Moldan of Duncansby, who despite their obvious Scandinavian names claimed to be kinsmen of the Scottish king. They saw the arrival of the newcomers as an opportunity to acquire loot, and clearly hoped to do this without casualties, so they gave the Njalssons' party the choice of going ashore and handing over their ship and goods, or being massacred. The merchants were about to surrender, but Helgi answered for them, announcing instead that the party chose to fight. Bard and Olaf were understandably angry at this, believing that they had no chance of success in a fight, but as they were now left with no choice they seized their weapons and prepared to sell their lives as dearly as they could. The local pirates opened the battle with a barrage of missiles, then closed and tried to board the merchants' ship. The first casualty was Olaf Ketilsson, killed by Snaekolf with a spear thrust, but Grim then struck Snaekolf with his spear and knocked him into the sea, though he was quickly rescued by his friends. Helgi and Grim, who, says the saga, 'were always there where the need was greatest', then joined forces and pushed the enemy back. Their enemies, obviously realising that their victims were a tougher proposition than they had thought, repeated their demand for them to surrender, but again they refused.

Just as the fight was about to resume, a fleet of longships was seen rowing round a headland on the south side of the fjord – probably Greenstone Point, which is on the direct route from the islands of Skye and Harris. There were ten ships, evidently equipped for war; shields were arrayed along their gunwales, and beside the mast of the leading vessel stood a man in a silk tunic, wearing a gilded helmet on his head and carrying a spear also decorated with gold. He was obviously a man of importance, and the warring factions prudently held their fire and waited until he came within hailing distance. The newcomer then asked Helgi the identities of the leaders on both sides, and on learning that he and Grim were the sons of Njal from Iceland he introduced himself as Kari, son of Solmund, coming from the Hebrides. He knew Njal by reputation, and on that account he agreed to help the merchants against their assailants. So the fight began again, but now all the advantages were with the Njalssons and their friends. Not only did Kari have a powerful retinue with him, but he also quickly proved himself to be a deadly fighter in his own right. We are told that he leaped onto Snaekolf's ship, at which Snaekolf swung at him with his sword, but Kari jumped backwards over a boom that was presumably hanging from the mast, and his assailant's blade struck this and became stuck. As Snaekolf struggle to free it Kari cut off his arm, a wound from which he died on the spot. Grjotgard then threw a spear at Kari, but he jumped over it and it missed him. The writer of *Njal's Saga* specialises in this sort of detailed description of combat, and this one, like the others, is probably largely fictional, but it is clear that Kari's intervention in the fight was decisive, whether or not he actually tipped the balance single-handed. By this time Helgi and Grim had joined Kari on the enemy's deck, and Helgi killed Grjotgard with a thrust from his sword. With their leaders dead, the rest of the enemy surrendered. The victors spared their lives, but took all their possessions before sailing off to anchor in the shelter of some nearby islands. It turned out that Kari had been collecting taxes in the Hebrides on behalf of his master, Earl Sigurd of Orkney, and the Njalssons accepted his invitation to accompany him to Orkney and meet the earl.

The third Battle of Skitten.

When Sigurd learned from Kari how well the Njalssons had fought in defence of their ship, he invited them to join his followers, and they stayed in Orkney over the following winter. But at the end of the season Helgi, who was said to have inherited the gift of second sight from his father, tipped off the earl that the Scots had invaded Caithness, killed his governor there and blockaded the Pentland Firth to prevent news of the coup reaching Orkney. Naturally Sigurd was sceptical at first, but he sent spies over to Caithness and discovered that, whatever the source of his information may have been, Helgi was right. Thereupon he raised a large army from all his island possessions and landed on the mainland. *Njal's Saga* describes the ensuing encounter as taking place at Duncansby Head, the most north-easterly point of the Scottish mainland just east of where John O'Groats now stands, but a number of scholars have come to the logical conclusion that it is the same encounter as that at Skitten Moor which is described in *Orkneyinga Saga*. Professor Cowan ('The Historical MacBeth', in Sellar, 1993) cites three 'well-respected authorities' in support of this idea, of whom the earliest is Anderson, in *Early Sources of Scottish History* (1922). It is easy to see why it has gained currency. *Orkneyinga Saga* mentions only one battle between Sigurd Hlodvirsson and the Scots, whereas if he had defeated them on two separate occasions, a work which aimed to glorify the earls of Orkney would surely have noted the fact. Duncansby and Skitten are only about ten miles apart, and from an Icelandic perspective the former, which in later centuries was a major naval base and a significant coastal landmark for navigators, would have been much more familiar. The names of the Scottish leaders are different in the two sources, but we need not necessarily expect a Norse writer to have been very well informed about the command structure of the enemy. In *Orkneyinga Saga* it was Finnleik who sent a challenge to Sigurd, whereas in *Njal's Saga* the 'Scots' are led by two earls named Hundi and Melsnati. It is generally assumed that, as in previous campaigns, these were the leading men of Moray with their local levies, rather than royal appointees in command of an army raised on behalf of the king of Scots. The political situation in Moray at this time is still poorly known, but Melsnati is obviously a version of Maelsnechtai, a name which is known to have been popular among the rulers of Moray (Cowan, 1993). The possible identification of Hundi with Finnleik has led to a great deal of speculation, which will be discussed in the next chapter.

Orkneyinga Saga's account of the actual battle is very brief. The armies of Sigurd and Finnleik deployed facing each other, and then both advanced to the attack. Sigurd's standard bearer was killed in the first clash, so the earl ordered another man to pick it up, but he too fell. Altogether he lost three standard bearers, but eventually the battle was won. Fortunately – and assuming that it really is describing the same conflict – *Njal's Saga* gives us a bit more information. The Scots had resorted to a stratagem, deploying a hidden detachment which emerged when battle was joined and charged into the Vikings' rear. This threw Sigurd's men into confusion and the attackers inflicted heavy losses, but the two Njalssons led a counterattack which drove them off. We are told that Grim and Helgi then advanced close to the earl's banner, but nothing is said here about its alleged magical powers, nor the deaths of the men who bore it. Kari Solmundarsson fought a duel with Earl Melsnati, who threw a spear at him, but Kari caught it and threw it back, killing the earl. Hundi and the remaining Scots then took flight, chased by the Orkney men. However, the saga says, they broke off the pursuit and returned to Orkney after learning that Melkolf, the Scottish king, was at Duncansby mustering another army. This seems highly unlikely. North-eastern Caithness at this date was firmly under Norse control, and the kings of Scots had neither the legal right nor the military power on the ground to raise troops there. We are given no further account of the operations of this force, and it was to be another two centuries before a Scottish royal army arrived again on the north coast. So if Melkolf was there at all it seems that he should be identified not with King Malcolm, but with another unidentified Moray warlord, who might have landed troops briefly at Duncansby in support of Hundi and Melsnati, but quickly reembarked them after their defeat.

Clontarf and the raven banner

The story of the raven banner does not end at Skitten Moor. *Orkneyinga Saga* follows its account of the battle with the story of how King Olaf Tryggvasson of Norway, who had been baptised as a Christian in the Scilly Isles, then sailed to Orkney and ordered Sigurd and all his subjects to follow his example. His argument was rather unchristian, but difficult for Sigurd to dispute: 'If you refuse, I'll have you killed on the spot.' So the earl underwent baptism, and 'all Orkney embraced the faith'. This method of conversion was by no means unusual at the time, as the new religion was seen as an important tool for strengthening royal control, but we can assume that for many years the influence of the new faith was fairly superficial. It certainly did not prevent the use of pagan symbols like Eithne's banner. Several years later, in 1014, Sigurd went to Ireland to fight in support of Sigtrygg Silkbeard, the Norse king of Dublin, against an army led by Brian Boru, the high king of Ireland. The campaign culminated in the Battle of Clontarf, which was fought on Good Friday, 23 April, on the coast just north of Dublin. It appears that the foreign Viking contingents, including those from Orkney and the Isle of Man, beached their ships in Dublin Bay and joined forces with the men from the town, with

Sigurd's men, according to *Njal's Saga*, advancing in the centre of the line. The resulting battle was a terrible slaughter even by the standards of the time, and its reverberations spread throughout northern Europe. It was commemorated not only in the Irish chronicles and the *Orkneyinga Saga*, but also in later works like *Njal's Saga*, which once again describes the fighting in (perhaps largely invented) detail. It is *Njal's Saga* that tells us most about the fate of Sigurd, and although it may not be entirely historical it probably preserves a genuine tradition, as the circumstances of the death of a man of such high rank must have been public knowledge. His new-found Christianity notwithstanding, Sigurd still went into battle with the magic banner beside him. A noted Irish warrior named Kerthjalfad, the foster son of King Brian, led the attack on Sigurd's division. He fought his way towards the man who carried the raven banner, killing everyone in his way, and cut him down. The flag was somehow retrieved and Sigurd ordered another man to take it, but he too was slain by the rampaging Kerthjalfad, along with everyone around him. The earl then asked Thorstein Hallsson to pick up the banner, but another Orkney man pointed out what must by then have been widely suspected, that everyone who took it was doomed to be killed. Thorstein therefore refused to obey the order, as did Hrafn the Red, who bluntly told Sigurd to carry the flag himself. So the earl removed it from its staff, wrapped it around his body, and returned to the fight. Needless to say, he was soon afterwards killed by a spear thrust, allegedly delivered by Brian's son Murchad. Sigurd is presumably the '*Siuchraid mac Loduir, iarla Innsi Orcc*' (ie. Sigurd son of Hlodvir, earl of the Orkney Islands) whom the *Annals of Ulster* also mention, in a rare corroboration of the saga narratives, as having fallen in the fighting.

What happened to the magic banner after the battle is not recorded. It would perhaps be fanciful to imagine that it somehow survived and later resumed its career, but Snorri Sturlason's history of the kings of Norway, *Heimskringla*, records a very similar tradition about Harald

Hardrada's raven flag, the 'Land Waster', which was flown at the Battle of Stamford Bridge in 1066, where Harald was defeated and killed by the English. According to Snorri, Harald told King Svein of Denmark that he regarded this banner as his most valuable possession, because of a prophesy that it would bring victory to the man before whom it was carried, and that this had always proved true ever since he had acquired it. We are not told where he had obtained the flag, but it seems from this remark that he was not its first owner. It should be mentioned that Paddy Griffith (1995) does not believe in the existence of these raven banners at all, although his reasons for this are unclear. In reality ravens feature prominently in pre-Christian Norse myth as the companions of Odin, while the fact that the real-life bird was well known to feast on corpses makes it an obvious choice for a battle flag. A 'banner which they called Raven' is mentioned by the *Anglo-Saxon Chronicle* as being captured from one of the sons of Ragnar Lodbrok in Wessex as early as 878. Of course it is not necessary to believe in magic to accept that such a standard could contribute significantly to the victory of the army that marched behind it – if only because the troops did believe in it – while at the same time endangering the life of its bearer. Not only would it inevitably attract the attention of the enemy, but as anyone who has carried a flag on a parade or march will know, it also requires constant attention to make sure that it flies properly, especially in poor weather, and does not droop in variable winds, get wet and wrap itself around the staff, or otherwise become invisible with potential risks to the army's morale. The flag bearer is therefore in no position to spot or defend himself against incoming missiles or similar threats.

After Sigurd

Earl Sigurd was just one of many prominent men on both sides who died that day at Clontarf. According to the sagas Sygtrygg ran away, followed by most of his men, though the Irish accounts say that he was never in the battle at all, but instead had watched the fighting from the walls of Dublin. The rest of the Viking line then crumbled and the foreign contingents tried to get back to their ships, but were left stranded as the tide had come in while they were fighting and floated off their ships. The Irish pursued them right into the sea, and few of them survived. The Manx commander Brodir, who had taken refuge in a wood, found Brian Boru in the rear, deserted by most of his men, who had joined in the pursuit, and killed him at the very moment of his victory. Brodir was then captured and, according to *Njal's Saga*, gruesomely executed. The same source goes on to recount a series of episodes which can hardly be historical, but which graphically illustrate the impact that the battle had as far away as the north of Scotland. The ghost of Earl Sigurd appeared and spoke to Harek, a man of his household, after which neither man was ever seen again. And on the morning of the battle, 400 miles away in Caithness, a man called Dorrud had a vision. Seeing twelve women going inside a building, he followed them and looked in through a window. He saw the women weaving on a loom made of the severed heads and intestines of men, while reciting a poem full of images of slaughter: 'Shafts will splinter, shields shatter... the heavens will be garish with the gore of men.'

This is the famous *Darradarliod* or 'Song of Dorrud', one of the skaldic poems which were frequently incorporated into the saga texts, and which are generally thought to date from much nearer in time to the events concerned. Barbara Crawford (2013) quotes suggestions that this one might have been composed within a year or so of the Battle of Clontarf. Another of its verses has sometimes been seen as very significant in a Scottish context: 'The men who inhabited the outer headlands, will now be leaders in the lands.'

Naturally most commentators (for example Professor Robert Cook in his translation of *Njal's Saga*) have identified these dwellers on the headlands as the Vikings, but there are difficulties with this idea. The Norse earls of Orkney were already the masters of large tracts of land, and it had been a long time since their ancestors had been the sort of pirates who might have relied on fortifying remote headlands as bases for their raiding activities. And if this political change is to be regarded as a consequence of the Battle of Clontarf, the death of the earl and the massive loss of life among his followers can hardly have assisted their people's rise to power. It is more likely, given the context, that the prophecy was intended to foretell the breakdown of the existing Norse order. With Sigurd gone, new contenders for power might have been expected to arise among those elements which were previously marginalised – including, perhaps, the native Gaels, who did indeed gradually reassert their role in the mixed Norse-Celtic society of the north. But as it happened, the glory days of the earldom of Orkney were yet to come. Another earl who was to become known to posterity by the nickname of 'the Mighty' was about to take the fight to the Scots.

Visiting the battle sites

The route of the coastal road into Caithness is now followed by the A9 from Inverness to Latheron, and the A99 from Latheron to Wick and John O'Groats. The nearest villages to the presumed location of the Skitten Moor battlefield (approximate grid reference ND291570), Watten and Reiss, are both accessible from Wick along the A882 and the A99 respectively, and there is a good bus service to both. There is, however, nothing to mark the site, and although a good impression can be gained from the roads of the general nature of the terrain, it has not been precisely identified. It is possible to walk along Sinclair's Bay between the villages of Keiss, at the northern end, and Reiss about five miles to the south, and the suitability of the great expanse of sand there for landing longships can easily be appreciated. Its vulnerability in this respect was well understood in the Second World War, and because of the remoteness of the site the concrete anti-tank obstacles which were placed to deter a German landing are still to be seen. Duncansby Head, two miles east of John O'Groats, has spectacular views overlooking the Pentland Firth, but again the exact location of any battle fought there cannot be pinpointed. Both the A836 from Tain and the Inverness to Wick railway line run up Strath Oykel past the Kyle of Sutherland to Lairg, traversing the tenth-century frontier between Norse Caithness and Scottish Moray. A few remnants of the forests which once attracted the Viking shipbuilders here can still be seen along the route.

Sueno's Stone (grid reference NJ046595) is north-east of Forres, near the roundabout where the B9011 to Findhorn leaves the A96. Forres is on the A96 about 20 miles east of Inverness, from where there is a regular train service. The stone is now enclosed in a transparent protective housing, but the figures and battle scenes can still be viewed close up, and give a vivid impression of the Scottish troops that might have fought at battles like Skitten Moor.

Chapter 3

Thorfinn's War and the Battle of Torfness

Date: 11 August 1040
Location: Burghead, near Elgin, Moray
Combatants: Thorfinn the Mighty, Earl of Orkney, versus Duncan I,
  King of Scots
Outcome: Orkney victory

Thorfinn Sigurdsson was a son of Earl Sigurd the Stout, the victor of Skitten Moor, and a daughter of King Malcolm II of Scotland. Again the main source for his career is *Orkneyinga Saga*. After his father's death at Clontarf in 1014, the five-year-old Thorfinn was sent to be fostered by his grandfather Malcolm, while his half-brothers Sumarlidi, Brusi and Einar divided the earldom of Orkney between them. Sumarlidi died soon after his father and Einar, whom the saga describes as a greedy and ruthless bully, seized his share of the islands for himself. Thorfinn's claim to the land in question was backed by Malcolm, who installed him in Caithness and provided Scottish advisors to rule on his behalf – a dangerous development that would ultimately lead to the claim that the earls of Orkney held their mainland territories as vassals not of Norway, but of the kings of Scots. While in Caithness Thorfinn was joined by Thorkel Amundarsson, a farmer from Sandwick in Orkney who had been forced to flee after protesting against Einar's excessive taxes. Thorkel, who took over the role of guardian to the young Thorfinn and so was later to become known as Thorkel 'Fosterer', eventually returned to Orkney following a reconciliation arranged by

Brusi, but was tipped off by spies that Einar intended to ambush him. He therefore avoided the trap, and instead took Einar by surprise in his hall and killed him. With Einar out of the way a settlement was agreed in 1021 with King Olaf of Norway, according to which Brusi would rule two-thirds of the earldom and Thorfinn the remaining third, owing allegiance to Norway for his lands in the islands and to Scotland for those in Caithness. This lasted until after Brusi's death around 1031, when Thorfinn became sole ruler. He was now around 26 years old. *Orkneyinga Saga* describes him as tall and strong, though ugly, with black hair, sharp features, bushy eyebrows and a big nose. 'He did well in battle', we are told, 'for he was both a good tactician and full of courage.'

Thorfinn came into conflict with the Kingdom of Scotland a few years after the death of his grandfather, King Malcolm. *Orkneyinga Saga* tells us that Malcolm's successor, a certain Karl Hundason, required the earl to pay tribute for Caithness, but Thorfinn argued (almost certainly contrary to the spirit of the settlement of 1021) that he had inherited the lordship outright from Malcolm and so was under no such obligation towards his successor. Malcolm II is known from Scottish sources to have been succeeded by another of his grandsons, Duncan, but many modern writers on the subject do not accept the obvious identification of Duncan with the mysterious Karl Hundason – an idea which was originally publicised by William Skene in *Celtic Scotland* (1880). The name is not otherwise known from contemporary sources, and it has been suggested, for example by Tom Muir (*Orkney in the Sagas*, Kirkwall, 2005), that it was in fact not the individual's proper name but an insult, meaning something like 'churl, son of a dog'. On the other hand Karl was a common and respectable Norse name at the time, and several men named Hundi are also attested in the sagas. One of these was Thorfinn's own brother, who had been fostered in Norway but had died young, so is unlikely to have left a son. Another Hundi, of course, was the Scottish earl who, along with Earl Melsnati, was said by *Njal's Saga* to have been defeated by Sigurd at the Battle of Duncansby or Skitten Moor (see Chapter 2). Several scholars have concluded that this Hundi should be identified with the Earl Finnleik whom the *Orkneyinga Saga* says was defeated by Sigurd in Caithness in what may be the same battle; consequently Karl Hundason, son of Hundi, has often been supposed to be Duncan's successor MacBeth, whose father's name, Findlaech, is clearly a variant of Finnleik. This identification has been made, for example, by Professor Cowan (1993), and Barbara Crawford (2013) describes it as 'the present consensus'. But the argument seems to depend on a number of unverifiable assumptions, and it is hard to avoid the suspicion that popular interest in MacBeth, stemming from Shakespeare's treatment of him, is partly responsible for its wide currency. One difficulty is that, as we saw in Chapter 1, Sigurd's battle against Finnleik cannot be certainly identified as the same one as the fight described in *Njal's Saga*. Even if both sagas are referring to the same battle, Finnleik and Hundi cannot necessarily be identified with each other – Melsnati, who is mentioned by *Njal's Saga* as a colleague of Hundi, is not noticed in *Orkneyinga Saga*, suggesting the possibility that there may have been other commanders besides Finnleik who were omitted from both accounts. More seriously, the writer of *Orkneyinga Saga* gives credence to a report that Karl was killed fighting against Thorfinn at the Battle of Torfness in 1040, while MacBeth ruled Scotland very successfully for another seventeen years, and his survival could hardly have gone unnoticed. It is more likely therefore, that Karl Hundason is indeed Duncan, who did die in 1040 – though not at the hands of Thorfinn. It is of course also possible that he was not a king of Scots at all, but merely another local leader in Moray otherwise unknown to history and elevated to the rank of king of Scotland by the saga writer, either through ignorance of the true power structure in the country, or deliberately in order to enhance Thorfinn's success against him.

Thorfinn and Rognvald

Although the dating of the Battle of Torfness seems secure from other sources, the chronology of *Orkneyinga Saga* is very confused around this time. It therefore seems that the long and complicated tale of the rivalry between Thorfinn and his fellow earl Rognvald, which the saga relates after the Karl Hundason episode, must in reality have extended over the whole period between 1035 and 1042, and may have considerable relevance for the events of 1040. In order to fully understand the background to the Torfness campaign, therefore, we need also to look at the Rognvald affair in detail. Not long after the death of Earl Brusi, his son Rognvald had appeared on the scene to contest Thorfinn's entitlement to the earldom. Rognvald was clearly a popular war leader; he is described by the saga as not only 'taller and stronger than other men' but 'outstandingly handsome and talented'. He had spent several years campaigning in Novgorod in Russia, where he had fought ten pitched battles, and while there he had been contacted by supporters of Magnus Olafsson, an illegitimate son of King Olaf, and persuaded to back his claim to the kingship of Norway. Magnus had lived in exile in Russia since his father's dethronement by Cnut in 1028, and after Olaf's death at the Battle of Stiklarstad in 1030 his supporters swore allegiance to him as king, although he was still only a child at the time. Magnus returned to Norway after Cnut's death in 1035. Cnut's son Svein then fled, and the eleven-year-old Magnus was proclaimed king. Rognvald was rewarded for his support with the title of joint earl of Orkney, control of a third of the islands, and three fully manned longships to support his claim. In addition another third of Orkney, which King Magnus claimed had belonged to his father, was granted to Rognvald in fee. So Rognvald sailed to Orkney and sent a message to Thorfinn informing him of the new arrangements. At first negotiations were surprisingly amicable. Thorfinn conceded his rival's right to the third given to him by

Magnus, but disputed that the other third had ever belonged to Olaf. He argued that it was his own by right, as an inheritance from his brother, but that he had been forced to acquiesce temporarily in Olaf's claim while the latter was on the throne. However, he was prepared to let Rognvald keep it in exchange for military aid in a forthcoming campaign against the Hebrideans and the Irish.

The following summer the two earls did campaign together in the Hebrides, where they won a decisive victory over the local warlords at Loch Vatten in Skye. On their return Thorfinn set up his headquarters in his old haunt in Caithness, while Rognvald resided in Orkney. *Orkneyinga Saga* says that this arrangement persisted for eight years, despite the attempts of troublemakers to set them against each other, and that successful joint raids were carried out in Wales and Ireland as well as in Scotland. One summer Thorfinn sailed as far as Galloway, in the far south-west of Scotland, but finding that the people had driven all their cattle inland for safety he sent a raiding party to take some from the English in Cumbria, on the other side of the Solway Firth. However, the party was surprised and massacred by the local people, who spared only a few survivors whom they sent back to Thorfinn with an insulting message. The earl returned to Caithness but came back the following year with a huge army raised from Orkney, Caithness, the Hebrides and Ireland, including contingents supplied by Rognvald. They landed in England, defeated the local levies in two pitched battles, and plundered far and wide. Arnor 'Jarlaskald', the 'Poet of the Earls' who travelled widely in the Viking world at this time composing poems in praise of its great men, sang of this campaign as a great victory. 'The English will ever remember this edge-storm' he exulted, though the *Anglo-Saxon Chronicle* never mentions it, no doubt because operations were in fact restricted to the remote north-west of the country. Place-name evidence indicates that there was substantial Norse settlement in Cumbria around this time, so Thorfinn's victims may well have been fellow Scandinavians rather than Englishmen. Once again, though, the saga's chronology is uncertain, because we are told that Thorfinn's attacks on England took place while the English king, Harthacnut, was in Denmark. However Harthacnut is known to have died in 1042, so these events must clearly have occurred less than eight years after Rognvald's return to Orkney in 1035 or 1036.

In any case it was soon after this enterprise that the joint earls finally fell out. The catalyst was the arrival of Thorfinn's wife's uncle, Kalf Arnason, who had had to flee from Norway and arrived in Orkney with a large following. Thorfinn found it difficult to support the newcomers on his reduced Orkney estates, so he asked Rognvald for the return of the third of the land which had supposedly belonged to Olaf. Rognvald refused, this time arguing that King Magnus had granted it to him. He also had a personal reason for reluctance to help Kalf, who had been one of those responsible for King Olaf's death. Thorfinn, however, was furious, and believing that now he would never recover his inheritance by peaceful means, he began to gather an army. He sent messengers to the Hebrides and Scotland to gather troops. Most of the Hebrideans had presumably sworn allegiance to him after their defeat at Loch Vatten. Exactly what the saga writer meant by 'Scotland' is not stated, but he adds that many of Rognvald's supporters advised him not to fight, since he could raise forces only from his two-thirds of Orkney, whereas Thorfinn controlled not only the remaining part of Orkney, but also 'Caithness, most of Scotland, and all the Hebrides as well'. The Scottish soldiers subject to his authority must therefore have been called up from places other than Caithness and the Hebrides, and it is possible that they would have been supplied by the nine Scottish earldoms which *Orkneyinga Saga* claims that Thorfinn temporarily controlled after his victory at Torfness (see below). In this case we must assume that the rift with Rognvald occurred soon after that battle, probably in 1041.

Despite the disparity in strength Rognvald was determined to fight, so he sailed to Norway to seek the backing of King Magnus. In this he was successful, and he returned not only with a large and well-equipped Norwegian army, but also with an offer of amnesty to Kalf Arnason if he would support him. Rognvald first gathered his forces in Shetland, then sailed south, intending to land in Caithness, but Thorfinn's fleet met him in the Pentland Firth and a battle was fought at sea. The saga gives the location as 'off Roberry', which is probably Rose Ness in south Mainland. Thorfinn, we are told, had sixty ships, but apart from his own flagship most of them were small, while his opponent's thirty vessels were larger. It seems that even at this early date the gradual evolution of the smaller Hebridean birlinn was under way, as ships from the Western Isles are routinely described as being outmatched by those built in Norway. Among the crew on Thorfinn's ship was the poet Arnor, whose verses on the subject are quoted extensively in *Orkneyinga Saga*. Kalf arrived with six of his own ships, which were also of Norwegian manufacture, and which appear from the saga's account to have been even bigger than most of Rognvald's, but at first he kept them out of the battle. When the fighting began Rognvald's men had the advantage because of the size and height of their ships, and Thorfinn suffered heavy losses. His own vessel put up fierce resistance but was eventually flanked and grappled from both sides after its smaller escorts had been put out of action. However, his men managed to cut the grappling ropes and escape to the nearby shore, where they unloaded seventy dead, as well as the non-combatant Arnor, and others too seriously wounded to continue. The remaining crew then managed to row out to join Kalf, whom Thorfinn persuaded to join him. Kalf then returned with Thorfinn to the fray, just in time to save the survivors of Thorfinn's fleet from being wiped out. By this time, if not before, it appears that Rognvald had had most of his ships roped together to form a stable fighting platform in typical Viking style. Thorfinn rowed straight up to Rognvald's vessel, while Kalf's six big ships bore down on the other enemy ships and his men quickly began to board and capture them, thanks to their greater height. Seeing this, Rognvald's Norwegians began to cut the ropes which bound their ships and flee. Arnor was scathing about the courage of the Norwegian contingent, claiming that if Rognvald had raised an army from Shetland instead he could have won the battle and conquered the whole country. As it was he was obliged to cut the grappling ropes that his enemies had attached to his flagship, just as Thorfinn had done earlier in the battle, and make his escape back to Norway.

Thorfinn followed up his victory by hunting down the survivors of Rognvald's men, who had scattered throughout the islands. Those who surrendered and swore allegiance to the earl were spared, but many others were killed. Thorfinn then took up residence in Orkney and sent Kalf Arnason to govern the Hebrides on his behalf. But Rognvald had not given up, and at the beginning of the following winter he returned unexpectedly with a single ship. No fleet would normally sail at that time of year, but he reasoned that one vessel with a picked crew had a good chance of landing undetected, and would be able to make its escape more quickly if anything went wrong. So he arrived in Shetland, where he learned that Thorfinn was staying in a certain house in Orkney, with only a small force to guard him. Sailing straight to Orkney, he achieved complete surprise and had surrounded the house and blocked all the doors before Thorfinn was aware of his presence. Then the attackers set fire to the house, at which point there was nothing that Thorfinn could do but try to negotiate. Rognvald's reply to a request for quarter was that the women and slaves could leave, but that the men who fought for Thorfinn 'would be better off dead'. The house was burnt to ashes and Rognvald assumed that Thorfinn had died in the fire along with his men, but in fact the earl had broken through a wooden partition wall and escaped under cover of the smoke, carrying his wife in his arms. As the night was very dark the couple were able to get to a boat undetected and row across to Caithness, where they were hidden by friends.

Rognvald set up his headquarters at Kirkwall, and believing that his rival was dead he devoted his time to feasting. Just before Christmas he went with a party of men to Papa Stronsay, a small outlying island in the north-east of Orkney, to fetch malt for brewing ale, and it was there that Thorfinn turned the tables on him. In a remarkable exhibition of carelessness Rognvald allowed himself to be trapped inside a house just as had happened to Thorfinn. Thorfinn's men had heaped a pile of wood in front of the door and set fire to it, but when a man in a long nightshirt appeared from inside he was not at first recognised, and it was only when he vaulted over the wood and ran into the darkness that Thorfinn realised that he must have been Rognvald. He despatched men to catch him, and they split up into groups and searched the nearby shoreline. It was Thorfinn's old henchman, Thorkel the Fosterer, who found him hiding among the rocks, betrayed by the yapping of a lap dog he was carrying. The saga writer says that Rognvald was still extremely popular and no one else was willing to harm him, but Thorkel had no hesitation in killing him on the spot. Thorfinn then slew the rest of his rival's men on the island and took their ship back to Kirkwall, with Rognvald's shields still decorating the gunwales. He was thus able to arrive at his destination without exciting suspicion, and most of Rognvald's supporters came out to meet him unarmed. Thirty of the men whom Magnus had sent from Norway were massacred, just one being spared to take the news to the king.

Thorfinn and Karl

To return to the activities of the mysterious Karl Hundason, it seems that in the year or so before 1040 he was making a determined effort to take control of the northern mainland, perhaps deliberately taking advantage of Thorfinn's preoccupation with Rognvald. Karl appointed his nephew, a man called Muddan, as earl of Caithness, and sent him north with an army which the saga says was raised in Sutherland – by which no doubt is meant the south-eastern part of what is now the county of Sutherland, along the Dornoch Firth, where Norse settlement had been sparse and most of the people were probably still loyal to the rulers of Moray. Thorfinn mustered his own followers in Caithness, and was joined once again by his faithful ally Thorkel Amundason. Thorfinn and Rognvald were supposedly on good terms at this time, but it is noteworthy that we do not hear anything of Rognvald's participation in the campaign. Nevertheless, Thorfinn was obviously able to recruit enough men for his purpose, because when Muddan learned of the strength of the forces arrayed against him he declined to risk a battle and retired; the saga says that the invaders 'rode back to Scotland', suggesting that they were a fast-moving mounted raiding party rather than a serious army of conquest, which would surely have included large numbers of infantry. Thorfinn followed up his success, and according to the saga 'conquered' Sutherland and Ross and raided extensively in Scotland before returning to Caithness. There he established a base at Duncansby, with five fully manned longships, in readiness for Karl Hundason's next move. When Muddan reported the defeat to Karl, the latter decided on a more ambitious two-pronged attack, advancing up the east coast himself with eleven longships, while Muddan was sent back to Caithness by an inland route – presumably the path up the Strath of Kildonan mentioned in Chapter 2 – to threaten Thorfinn from the west. Muddan had also at some point journeyed to Ireland, where he had many kinsmen, to raise more troops, but the impression gained from the saga account is that his force was not large.

Karl's fleet arrived off Caithness just as Thorfinn was setting sail for Sandwick to rendezvous with Thorkel, whom he had instructed to muster his troops. The Scots spotted the sails of the Norse fleet and went in pursuit, but Thorfinn, who was still unaware of the approach of his enemy, anchored off the headland of Deerness on the mainland of Orkney to await a response to his message to Thorkel. At dawn the following morning Karl's more numerous fleet could be seen closing in, trapping the earl against the shore. Realising that he would have to surrender or fight, Thorfinn ordered an immediate advance, encouraging his men by saying that the Scots would not stand up to the pressure of hard fighting. The earl's five ships grappled together with his enemy's eleven, and the saga tells us that the fight was long and brutal, with much slaughter on both sides. Thorfinn brought his ship up to Karl's and boarded it, apparently alone, cutting his way through the enemy from the forecastle to the stern. Seeing that the Scots' resistance was weakening, he called for his men to join him, and as they did so Karl ordered his own men to cut the ropes that held the ships together so that he could make his escape. It was too late: the earl's men had already attached their own grappling hooks, with which they held their prize in place while they cleared the deck, Thorfinn's banner at their head. Karl and the few surviving crew abandoned ship and managed to scramble on board another vessel which was rowing away, and the Scots retreated in confusion, with Thorkel's ships in pursuit.

Karl sailed back to the Moray Firth, and Thorfinn, joined by Thorkel, went after him. The Scots king managed to escape inland and started raising a new army, while the Norsemen plundered along the coast. Then news was brought to Thorfinn that Muddan had occupied Thurso, at the mouth of the river of the same name ('Thor's River') on the north coast of Caithness, and was waiting there for his Irish allies to arrive. So while the earl continued his raids on the Moray coast, Thorkel the Fosterer secretly went ashore with some of his men and marched to Thurso. The saga says that the people living along the way were all loyal to Thorkel and his master, and so no intelligence of his movements reached Muddan until it was too late. Muddan was asleep in an upstairs room in the town when the Orkney men arrived under cover of darkness and began to set fire to the buildings. This account, incidentally, tells us that Thurso was already a substantial town at this time, including two-storey houses built at least partly of wood. No trace of the early medieval settlement now survives, but it presumably clustered around the bay, a sheltered anchorage which features in *Orkneyinga Saga* on several later occasions and was clearly of great strategic value. There was a castle there in the thirteenth century, but there is no suggestion in the saga that the town had been provided with any walls or other defences in Thorfinn's day. When Muddan realised that his house was on fire he jumped off the balcony to the ground, but Thorkel was waiting for him there and cut off his head with a single blow. There seems to have been no further resistance; some of Muddan's men surrendered, the saga tells us, while the rest fled. Thorkel granted quarter to most of those who yielded, but 'a good many' were killed, perhaps overtaken as they tried to escape.

The Battle of Torfness

Thorkel then returned to Moray to join a grateful Earl Thorfinn, who was now free to focus on the last remaining threat – Karl Hundason and his newly raised army. This army included men from throughout Scotland as far south as Kintyre, as well as Muddan's Irish relatives, who had marched to join the king on learning of their kinsman's death. Unfortunately we cannot tell from the saga what part, if any, Thorfinn's rival Rognvald played in the war. Depending on the exact sequence of events he might have been fighting on Thorfinn's side, or against him, or even have already been dead. Most likely he remained on the sidelines in Orkney, perhaps awaiting the outcome before making his move. In the end it was the Scots who advanced to bring Thorfinn to battle, an encounter which *Orkneyinga Saga* says was fought at a place called Torfness or 'Turf Point', where in the early tenth century Earl Einar Rognvaldsson had discovered the use of peat as fuel. The location of Torfness has been much discussed, with scholarly opinion divided among three possible sites, all of which might potentially have yielded deposits of peat. The furthest north of these is at Tarbat Ness, a headland on the south side of the Dornoch Firth near the village of Portmahomack. Another is at Pitgaveny, on the shores of Loch Spynie about three miles north of the city of Elgin in Moray, while the third is seven miles north-west of Elgin, on the southern shore of the Moray Firth at Burghead. Pitgaveny is perhaps the easiest of the three to dismiss. It is usually identified with Bothnagowan, the place where, according to the *Annals of Tigernach*, King Duncan was killed by MacBeth, but this is several miles inland, and would hardly have been referred to by the saga writer as a 'ness', which was the old Norse word for a headland. Tarbat Ness is at first sight a much more promising location, and has been favoured by many modern authorities, including Barbara Crawford. However, this site is at the extreme northern tip of the Easter Ross peninsula, at least ten miles from any useable road leading south, and so would hardly be a useful base for anyone operating against the Scots. An army landed there would be hardly any better placed to threaten Moray than if it had stayed in Caithness, and Thorfinn would surely have used his seaborne mobility to get as close as possible to his objective. In the aftermath of the battle he is also described by *Orkneyinga Saga* as marching south, apparently overland, through eastern Scotland as far as Fife – something which would be very difficult to do from Tarbat Ness.

The most likely site for the battle is therefore near Burghead, which today is a small town built on the site of an old Pictish fortification on a headland which juts out into the Moray Firth. The Pictish remains were mostly destroyed by building work in the nineteenth century, but a map of the site drawn by General William Roy in 1793 survives, and it indicates that in pre-Viking times this was probably the largest promontory fort in Scotland. James Gray (1922) remarks that peat, 'though now submerged', is found 'in abundance' at Burghead. The dearth of later archaeological finds has led most scholars to believe that it was abandoned around the ninth century, probably because its coastal location made it too vulnerable to Viking raids, but recent excavations have shown that there is still a lot to discover underneath the nineteenth-century debris. A particularly significant find was a coin of Alfred the Great of Wessex, suggesting that the fort was still occupied, and perhaps still involved in long-distance trade, as late as the end of the ninth century (*Current Archaeology*, 20 September 2017). It might have been one of the sites in 'Argyll, Moray and Ross' which were captured by Sigurd the Mighty according to *Orkneyinga Saga*, and even if it was abandoned for a time, it is likely that the earls of Orkney were well aware of its strategic value, and could have temporarily reoccupied it when the military situation required. The site has a good beach for landing ships on the western side, and it was protected in the Middle Ages not just by its fortifications and its elevated position, guarded by the sea on three sides, but also by extensive marshes on the inland approaches. Nevertheless, it offered relatively easy access to the rich lands and towns of Moray, in stark contrast to Tarbat Ness.

Orkneyinga Saga says that the Scottish army outnumbered Thorfinn's men, but he nevertheless advanced to meet it. If the earl was indeed based at Burghead, the battle must have taken place on what was then the flat, low-lying and marshy ground just inland, as the fortifications of the town itself appear to have played no part in it. Gray – apparently citing a local tradition – states that the battle was fought at Standing Stane in the parish of Duffus, just over three miles east of Burghead. The Canmore website (www.canmore. org.uk) identifies another standing stone near Longhillock, around three miles south of the fort (grid reference NJ136643), as Torfness, and classes it as a 'Battle site, period unassigned'. Neither location seems to be based on anything more than the usual tradition that any standing stone must have been erected to commemorate a battle, and the best we can say is that the site was within a few hours' march of Burghead, possibly within sight of the fortifications, but equally possibly several miles to the south or east. It appears that both sides were on foot, and we know that when battle was joined Thorfinn was marching at the head of his troops, conspicuous in a golden helmet, with a sword at his waist and a long spear held in both hands. Probably both sides advanced towards each other in a single line consisting of several ranks drawn up in close order, as was usual in that period. The Irish account of *The War of the Gaedhil with the Gaill* claims that at Clontarf the Irish troops were drawn up in such close order that a four-horsed chariot could have been driven from one end of the battle line to the other on their heads. As discussed in Chapter 1, it is likely that as Thorfinn approached the enemy line he was greeted by the terrifying sound of large numbers of horns being sounded in unison. It is clear, however, that the Orkney host was by no means intimidated, because the initiative seems to have been Thorfinn's from the start. The saga tells us that his first onslaught was aimed at the Irish contingent in Karl Hundason's army, which appears to have been unable to stand the shock. If they were native Irishmen and not Scandinavians from Dublin this is understandable, as the Irish seem at this date to have been relatively lightly equipped. According to *The War of the Gaedhil with the Gaill*, by the time of the Battle of Clontarf in 1014 some of the chiefs and leading men among the Irish contingents already possessed heavy axes designed to penetrate the mail armour of the Norsemen, but these would probably have been a small minority in the eleventh century. The noblemen may have been equipped as lightly armed cavalry, but the rank and file generally fought on foot, relying on javelins and even – according to Gerald de Barri, writing a hundred years later – stones as missiles.

They lacked armour, and so relied heavily on their superior mobility in difficult terrain; Gerald, for example, tells us that they had no castles, but 'use the woods as their fortresses and the marshes as their entrenchments'. Even as late as the fourteenth century, Froissart describes the Irish as preferring to scatter when hard pressed, and as being able to outrun even mounted knights over the boggy terrain of their native country. At Torfness, therefore, the Irishmen might have been deployed either as part of Karl's close-order battle line, or in front of the Scots army as a screen of skirmishers, but either way they were evidently exposed to the Norse onslaught without having the freedom of movement which their tactics required. The area was not marshy enough to hamper the close-fighting tactics of the Orkney men, because Thorfinn's attack quickly attained its object. The saga says that the Irish 'fell back at once' and never returned to the fray. Karl Hundason then brought up his main body behind his banner to meet Thorfinn, but was beaten after a hard fight and eventually turned to flee. The saga writer obviously did not know what happened to Karl after the battle, as he adds simply that 'some say he was killed there'. This seems a strange remark, because if Thorfinn or one of his men had brought down the king of Scots we would expect them to have recognised him by his expensive war gear and to have boasted later of their achievement – unless, of course, Karl had thrown away in his flight any regalia by which he could be identified.

In fact we have a good idea of what did happen to Karl Hundason, because the eleventh-century *Chronica Clara* of Marianus Scotus tells us that King Duncan was killed 'by his general MacBeth, son of Findlay', on the day before the Feast of the Assumption in 1040. According to the *Annals of Tigernach* this took place at Bothnagowan, about eight miles south-east of Burghead, so Duncan could have arrived there within a few hours of the battle. Fordun gives further details, though his source is unclear. He says that Duncan was wounded in a blacksmith's shop (Bothnagowan means 'blacksmith's

The Kyle of Sutherland, looking north-west towards Bonar Bridge. The Kyle, and the River Oykel which empties into it (middle distance, centre left) marked the southern boundary of Norse territory in the time of Earl Sigurd the Mighty. Remnants of the extensive forests which made this area so attractive to Viking shipbuilders can still be seen along the shores. (*VisitScotland*)

Although eroded, the figures carved on the ninth or tenth-century Sueno's Stone, near Forres in Moray, are an important source for the appearance of early Scottish warriors. The name of the monument derives from its supposed association with Svein Forkbeard, King of Denmark from 986 to 1014, but this is not supported by modern studies. (*VisitScotland*)

All photos taken by the author unless otherwise credited.

The broch at Dun Carloway on the Isle of Lewis is one of the best preserved of the Pictish stone towers which are a prominent feature of the coastal districts of northern and western Scotland. The double-walled construction, with a stairway between the inner and outer walls giving access to an upper floor, can be clearly seen. Although windowless and so apparently vulnerable to surprise attack, some of these structures were still being used for defence until the sixteenth century. (*VisitScotland*)

A view westwards across the Flow Country of Caithness towards the mountains of Sutherland, with the line of the modern railway in the foreground. Although fairly flat, the region is an enormous uninhabited wilderness of peat bogs, which must have been an insuperable obstacle to a mediaeval army attempting to approach the settled coastal districts of Caithness from the landward side. (*VisitScotland*)

This view along the exposed and rocky coast of Caithness shows the difficulty of landing ships, and emphasises the value of the few sandy beaches like Sinclair's Bay near the battle site of Skitten Moor. (*VisitScotland*)

The flat moorland inland from Sinclair's Bay, Caithness, shrouded in a characteristic sea mist or 'haar'. Somewhere in this bleak and featureless landscape was the rendezvous known as Skitten Moor, where Scots and Vikings clashed repeatedly.

Loch Broom, the probable scene of the Njalssons' encounter with pirates before they joined Sigurd the Stout for the Third Battle of Skitten Moor. The mountains of Wester Ross are in the background.

Thurso Bay, the site of the main Viking settlement on the north coast of the Scottish mainland, seen from the west. It was here that Thorkel 'Fosterer' surprised and killed Muddan before the Battle of Torfness.

The beach to the west of the promontory at Burghead. This is probably the place where Thorfinn the Mighty beached his longships before joining battle with Karl Hundason at Torfness.

Burghead today, looking south from the Pictish fortifications towards the site of the battle.

Duffus Castle, originally built by David I's protégé Freskin de Moravia in the mid-twelfth century, overlooks the plain near Burghead where the Battle of Torfness was fought two centuries earlier. (*VisitScotland*)

The fertile farmland of Mainland, Isles of Orkney. The offshore island in the background is the Brough of Birsay, where the earls of Orkney had their stronghold until the twelfth century. (*VisitScotland*)

The beach at Tankerness on Mainland, Orkney, with the modern settlement of the same name, the presumed site of Erlend's farm, in the background. The beach is still littered with large stones of the sort which Erlend loaded onto Earl Paul's ships for use as missiles in the battle.

A view eastwards across Deer Sound, the site of the sea battle off Tankerness.

Mull Head, seen at the mouth of Deer Sound from the shore near Tankerness.

Looking west down the Clyde from Braehead, with the Kilpatrick Hills of Dumbartonshire in the distance. It was by this route that Somerled's fleet sailed to the battle at Renfrew, and his army presumably came ashore somewhere along the south (i.e. left) bank near here.

The footpath along the River Clyde at the Braehead shopping centre near Renfrew. Somewhere near here, unmarked, is the place where Somerled the Great met his death.

The abbey on the Hebridean island of Iona, the site of a series of Viking attacks in the ninth century, and burial place of the kings of Scots. Somerled is also believed to have been interred here. (*VisitScotland*)

Strath Bran, west of Garve, in winter. Although the mountains in this vicinity are neither very high nor very steep, snow can lie for a significant portion of the year, contributing to the difficulty of campaigning in the region. (*VisitScotland*)

The eastern slopes of Ben Wyvis, overlooking Strath Garve, photographed from Dingwall. The Battle of Mam Garvia took place somewhere in these hills in July 1187.

Looking north-westwards along Glen Docherty, Wester Ross, towards Loch Ewe and the west coast. This is the most probable route by which the Hebridean and Irish troops fighting for the MacWilliams would have marched to their defeat at Mam Garvia. (*VisitScotland*)

Harald's Tower overlooking Thurso Bay. This monument was built on the site of an earlier chapel which is said to have marked the spot where Harald the Young was killed at the Battle of Clairdon.

The old ford across the Thurso River. Until the twentieth century this was the only reliable way of crossing from Clairdon on the east to Thurso on the west bank. This picture was taken in dry weather in May, but for much of the year the river is a far more formidable obstacle, and high water may have prevented reinforcements from Thurso from reaching the field at Clairdon by this route.

The battlefield of Clairdon from the landward side, with Harald's Tower on the horizon.

Looking out to sea from the mouth of the Thurso River, with Dunnet Head visible in the distance. It may have been here that the final act of the Battle of Clairdon was played out when the victorious Orkney men overtook the fugitives from Harald the Young's army.

The island of Great Cumbrae, seen across Fairlie Roads from the harbour at Largs. The Norwegian fleet was driven by a storm up this narrow channel on the eve of the battle.

A view of the town of Largs from the sea. It was probably somewhere on the ridge behind the town that the Norwegian advance guard led by Ogmund Kraekidants first deployed, and down these slopes that it was driven back to the beach by the Scottish charge. (*VisitScotland*)

Looking south along the beach at Largs, with the marina and the 'Pencil' in the distance. It was probably here that King Haakon's ships were driven aground and became the focal point of the fighting along the shore.

The 'Pencil' overlooking what is now Largs Marina at the southern end of the town. The monument was built in 1912 to commemorate the battle, which probably reached its climax among the grounded Norwegian ships on the beach in the middle distance. (*VisitScotland*)

Largs is the only one of the battles discussed in this book which is actually commemorated on the site. The Vikingar Centre on the north side of town features a reconstructed Viking ship, exhibitions and other attractions such as costumed storytellers. (*VisitScotland*)

shop' in Gaelic), and died at nearby Elgin. This tradition was obviously known to King Alexander II, who in 1235 founded a chapel in Elgin Cathedral where masses could be sung for Duncan's soul. It can only be an assumption, but it makes sense to suppose that Duncan was killed in a power struggle following his ignominious flight from the battle with Thorfinn, and that the murder occurred soon enough after the battle to give rise to a rumour, picked up by the saga writer, that he had not survived it. He may of course have been wounded and carried from the field, which would have added to the confusion about his fate. On the other hand, if he had fled and abandoned his army to be defeated, this would have given MacBeth an additional motive to overthrow him. The Feast of the Assumption took place on 14 August, so we can assume that the Battle of Torfness was fought on or a few days before this date. The poet Arnor, quoted in *Orkneyinga Saga*, refers to it as a 'Monday combat', while according to the Julian calendar in use at this time 13 August, the presumed day of Duncan's death, was a Wednesday. It therefore seems likely that Duncan survived his defeat by two days: just enough time for his disillusioned general MacBeth to organise a coup.

Thorfinn and MacBeth

In the view of the writer of the *Orkneyinga Saga* the victory of Torfness was decisive, at least in the short term, because Thorfinn came close to dominating most of Scotland in the aftermath. He pursued the fugitives 'deep into Scotland', then marched on as far as Fife, accepting the surrender of the people. This certainly sounds like more than a Viking raid, but the earl's precise aim can only be conjecture. In his obituary in the saga Thorfinn is said to have conquered nine Scottish earldoms, though their locations are not stated. If the claim relates to this campaign, as is likely, it implies that at one point he controlled the entire east coast from Caithness to Fife, receiving the formal submission of most of its earls or mormaers. It seems improbable, though, that he ever intended to hold all this territory permanently. When he reached Fife he was clearly worried about the risk of leaving his northern possessions undefended, because he sent Thorkel the Fosterer back to the north with part of the army. This may be related to one of the episodes of bad feeling which the saga says occurred between Thorfinn and Rognvald before the final rift. When the Scots realised that he had divided his forces, many of them renounced their allegiance and took up arms again. The saga says that a fresh Scottish army took the field, but we are not told who had raised it, and it was clearly badly led. When they arrived on the field of battle and saw that the Norsemen were deployed and ready for them the Scots hesitated, surrendering the initiative, and then scattered as soon as Thorfinn advanced to the attack. The earl regarded this revolt as treason and ordered the surrounding countryside to be devastated as a punishment. His men went from one village to another, burning all the houses, killing all the adult men they could find, and driving off the women and children as slaves. 'Thrice in one short summer he struck them' says Arnor. Thorfinn then returned to Caithness, probably in order to pursue his unfinished dispute with Rognvald, but incidentally giving MacBeth, who had now seized the Scottish throne, the breathing space he needed to secure his position.

Orkneyinga Saga goes on to tell the story of how Thorfinn managed to avoid retribution for the subsequent killing of Rognvald until after King Magnus's death in 1047, and eventually became reconciled with his successor Harald II Sigurdsson (the famous Harald 'Hardrada' who was to die in battle against the English at Stamford Bridge in 1066). Thorfinn then felt secure enough to go on a pilgrimage to Rome, where the Pope gave him absolution for all his sins, and returned to Orkney to rule successfully until his death in 1064. There seems to have been no further trouble with the Scots. The other surviving protagonist in the events of 1040, MacBeth, is of course better known as a Shakespearean villain than as a historical figure, but it seems that he was sufficiently closely related to the royal family to have a plausible claim to the throne. His father Finnleich, as we have seen, may also have been a mormaer of Moray, and Professor Cowan (1993) has produced a speculative family tree which suggests that he may have been the grandson of King Kenneth II through his mother. We do know that he took the throne after the death of Duncan and reigned, largely peacefully, for another seventeen years. Like Thorfinn he visited Rome on a pilgrimage in or around the year 1050. Professor Cowan (1993) has speculated that the two men might even have travelled together, which is an intriguing idea, if unproveable. (The historical novelist Dorothy Dunnett went so far as to suggest, in her impressively researched book *King Hereafter*, that Thorfinn and MacBeth were in fact the same person. The arguments for and against this thesis are too involved to rehearse here, but I have found no academic historian who takes the suggestion seriously.) Perhaps more plausible is a theory that Thorfinn may have visited the Archbishopric of Cologne and introduced some of its sophisticated financial and administrative arrangements into Orkney (Williams & Bibire, 2004). The Cologne silver penny was very stable in this period and was regarded as something of an international standard. An ounce was made up of eighteen such pennies, and in Orkney the traditional territorial unit, the ounceland, which was the basis of the 'leidang' system of military recruitment, comprised eighteen pennylands. This was in contrast to the situation in western Scotland, where a similar system prevailed but the ounceland consisted of twenty pennylands. Only one Cologne penny has actually been found in Orkney to date – in the Burray hoard, which slightly predates Thorfinn – but his European travels make him an obvious candidate for this sort of innovation. This does not necessarily mean that Thorfinn introduced the system of ouncelands and pennylands, but Barbara Crawford suggests that the division of the ounceland into pennylands may have occurred around this time. In any case it appears that Thorfinn did put the administration of the earldom on a more formal basis. This unaccustomed emphasis on formal government and, no doubt, the efficient raising of taxes, may have strengthened the authority of the earl, but it may also be one reason why, as *Orkneyinga Saga* tells us, people in the regions that he had conquered found his rule 'very oppressive' and broke away after his death.

Meanwhile, the kingdom of Scotland was clearly just as prosperous under the rule of MacBeth; the *Melrose Chronicle* notes the 'productive seasons' for which his reign was remembered, and when he visited Rome he was rich enough to be able to scatter money 'like seed'. The remark about productive seasons should not be taken merely as a comment on the weather. Given the sacral nature of Scottish kingship, which is discussed further in Chapter 6, the implication is clearly that MacBeth was endorsed by God as a benevolent and legitimate ruler. But by the time he returned from his pilgrimage his enemies were already closing in. In 1054 he seems to have fought off a dangerous invasion by Earl Siward of Northumbria, which may have been related to an attempt by the English king Edward the Confessor to interfere with the Scottish succession. Three years later, however, he was defeated at Lumphanan in Aberdeenshire by Malcolm Canmore, a son of the late King Duncan, and soon after this both MacBeth and his stepson and successor Lulach were dead. Malcolm took the throne as Malcolm III, founding the dynasty which was to rule Scotland until the end of the thirteenth century, and it was not long before the agents of Canmore propaganda were at work on MacBeth's reputation. Thorfinn's reputation fared rather better; *Orkneyinga Saga* concludes its account of his life with the remark that 'it is said on good authority that he was the most powerful of all the earls of Orkney.'

The battle sites today

Burghead (grid reference NJ109691) is about eight miles north-east of Elgin, and although the actual spot where the battle was fought has not been identified, the journey from Elgin on the B9012 via Duffus will give a good impression of the terrain over which it was fought. An excellent panoramic view of the land to the west can be obtained from the ruins of Duffus Castle (grid reference NJ189672), which are signposted from the road, and are open to the public and free to visit. The castle was built in the wake of the royal defeat of the men of Moray at the Battle of Stracathro in 1130, and there is no evidence that a fortification existed on the site as early as Thorfinn's day. There is a fairly frequent bus service to Burghead from Elgin, which is accessible by rail from Inverness. The town itself is in an impressive location overlooking the Moray Firth, and the ruins of the earthworks on the seaward side of the Pictish fort can still be seen. There is an informative visitor centre, and it is also possible to visit a mysterious well which was apparently used at some point for baptism, but may also have been the water supply for the fort during the Viking occupation.

The Battle of Roberry between Thorfinn and Rognvald was fought at sea off Rose Ness at the mouth of Holm Sound in Orkney, about three miles east of where the Churchill Barriers now protect the entrance to the anchorage at Scapa Flow. A good view of the general area can be obtained from the A961, which traverses the causeway along the Churchill Barriers en route from Kirkwall to St Margaret's Hope on South Ronaldsay and is served by frequent buses from Kirkwall.

Chapter 4

A Fruitless Victory: Tankerness, 1136

Date: 1136
Location: Deer Sound, off Mainland, Orkney
Combatants: Earl Paul of Orkney versus Hebrideans led by Olvir, grandson of Frakokk
Outcome: Orkney victory

A century after Thorfinn's victory at Torfness, the political landscape in Scotland had changed significantly. Malcolm Canmore and his sons had ruled the kingdom since 1057 and the current king David I, who had been on the throne since 1124, was enthusiastically pursuing his father's policy of introducing feudal institutions and other modern ideas from England. In the long run the strengthening and centralisation of royal authority which this involved would be bad news for the independent rulers of Scotland's northern and western periphery. Orkney, however, was still subject not to Scotland but to Norway, and events were still very much driven by the old theme of rival claimants to the earldom, often set against each other by their overlords in Norway. It was an unfortunate habit of the Norwegian kings to assume that they could dispose of all or part of Orkney to reward their favourites as they pleased, but as the islands were a long way from Norway and the earls maintained their own military forces, this almost inevitably led to bloodshed. In a remarkable echo of the war between Thorfinn and Rognvald Brusason, the Battle of Tankerness was fought between Earl Paul Haakonsson, son of Earl Haakon who had ruled from 1104 until 1123, and a fleet campaigning in support of another Rognvald, also known by his alternative name of Kali Kolsson. The two rivals were both great-grandsons of Thorfinn the Mighty, but Paul could trace his descent through the male line, while Rognvald's claim was inherited through his mother, Gunnhild. More relevant, however, was that Rognvald had helped Harald, one of the claimants to the then disputed throne of Norway, to secure a victory in the recent civil war, and as a means of rewarding him without cost to himself the new king had granted him half of Orkney. Sometime in 1135 the king sent Rognvald's father, Kol Kalasson, to Orkney to order Paul to honour the gift and hand over half of his territory in the islands. Understandably Paul refused to obey, arguing that Rognvald had been scheming for a long time to supplant him and had clearly obtained the grant dishonestly.

Kol realised that the only way his king's command could be enforced was through war, so he sent envoys to Sutherland, where they sought the help of a landowner by the name of Frakokk Moddansdottir, the widow of Ljot of Sutherland. This Frakokk typified the blend of Norse and Gaelic culture which had now arisen on the frontiers of Caithness and Sutherland. According to *Orkneyinga Saga* she had been exiled to the mainland from Orkney on suspicion of attempting to murder Earl Paul by weaving a poisoned shirt as a gift for him: a rather unlikely allegation which may nevertheless reflect a genuine suspicion of disloyalty. She had extensive connections by blood and marriage with the northern Scottish nobility, including Earl Maddad of Atholl, an extensive inland territory in what later became northern Perthshire, south of the boundaries of Moray. Maddad was not only a powerful magnate in his own right, but a nephew of the late Scottish king Malcolm Canmore. Frakokk was also the sister of a certain Ottar Moddansson, who at this time was holding Thurso as a de facto independent 'earldom', although legally the town was still subject to Paul in Orkney. She was therefore able to raise a large number of troops from various localities, and she already had a strong motive for removing the earl from power. Kol offered Paul's half of Orkney to her and her grandson Olvir if they would help Rognvald, and they agreed to raise an army over the winter and rendezvous in Orkney at midsummer the following year.

Rognvald, who was no doubt kept informed of these negotiations and intended to rely on Frakokk's assistance, set sail from Norway in the spring of 1136 with only five or six ships, manned by what the *Orkneyinga Saga* calls a 'small but select band' of men. At midsummer he arrived in Shetland, but was overtaken by a gale and forced to take shelter on the island of Yell. Meanwhile Frakokk and Olvir had been recruiting in the Hebrides, but had collected only about a dozen of the small local ships, which the saga describers as 'poorly manned'. They set out for Orkney as agreed, but were delayed by unfavourable winds. It is clear from the saga's account that once they had all put to sea there was no further communication between Rognvald and his allies, but Paul, who was based at Westness on the island of Rousay in Orkney, was well informed about the movements of both of their fleets. A glance at the map will show the strategic problem that Rognvald faced: to sail directly across the open ocean between Shetland on the one hand, and the Hebrides and Sutherland on the other, was a very risky proposition, and there was a good chance that the fleets would miss each other, especially if the winds were unfavourable. The only realistic plan was the one which he adopted, to use the Orkney Islands as a rendezvous and rallying point. But Orkney was the heartland of the enemy and – precisely because all shipping had to pass through it – the ideal place for gathering intelligence. At a conference held at Westness, several of Paul's advisors recommended that he open negotiations with either Rognvald or Olvir in the hope of breaking up their alliance, while others suggested waiting until they could raise more men from Caithness. Paul, however, had made up his mind to fight with the forces he had, and the next day he prepared to sail for Shetland from the anchorage at Tankerness in Deer Sound, a large sheltered bay on the Mainland about five miles south-east of Kirkwall.

Tankerness

Earl Paul's intention at that stage was to intercept Rognvald before he could join forces with the Hebrideans. A few more men from the islands of Orkney were gathered up overnight, but the earl's followers had only five ships between them, and no more were to be found at such short notice. Then, at dawn the next day, ten or twelve longships were reported sailing north across the Pentland Firth. Realising that these must be Frakokk's men, Paul quickly changed his plans and made preparations to attack them, but before his ships could get underway the enemy were seen rounding Mull Head on the eastern side of the sound. The saga does not explicitly say so, but it is obvious from the map that the Hebrideans, who were under the command of Frakokk's grandson Olvir, had already won the battle of manoeuvre, bottling up Paul's fleet in the bay and forcing it to accept battle. But Viking sea fights were not won by clever manoeuvres. Paul responded by lashing his ships together to form a fighting platform, which he packed with every man who could find room on board. The saga lists the captains of the ships as Eyvind Melbrigdason, Olaf Hrolfsson from Gairsay, Thorkel 'Flayer', and Sigurd, with Earl Paul himself commanding the fifth. Olaf is later described as manoeuvring independently, so it seems that it was only the remaining four ships that were actually roped together. The occupant of the farm at Tankerness, Erlend, offered to bring his sons and fight with the earl, but the ships were already too crowded, so he tasked them with gathering rocks from the beach for use as missiles. Large stones were often used in this way in sea fights; not only could they do a lot of damage at short range, but they were also freely available and more easily replaced than costly spears and arrows, which were unlikely to be recoverable if they missed their targets.

No sooner had Paul completed his preparations than the Hebrideans advanced to the attack. Olvir's own vessel was larger than the others, and he laid it alongside Paul's ship and attempted to board. Meanwhile Olaf Hrolfsson advanced to meet the enemy, and from the higher vantage point of his own ship he managed to clear the decks of the first three he encountered. But Olvir's onslaught was so ferocious that he succeeded in driving Paul's men back from the bows of the earl's ship and boarding it. The defenders clustered around the mast; the saga mentions that they occupied a 'raised deck', which was obviously higher than the bows because Paul jumped down from it to lead a counterattack. Olvir then threw a spear at the earl, who took it on his shield but was knocked down by the impact. 'There was a lot of shouting', says the saga, which is not surprising as this encounter between the rival leaders had the potential to decide the battle. An army was always very vulnerable to confusion and panic if its commander was out of action, while if Paul were to be killed the issue of the succession to the earldom would be decided on the spot. No doubt Olvir and his men rushed forward at once to take advantage of their opportunity, but one of Paul's leading retainers, a man named Svein 'Breast Rope', quickly picked up one of the heavy stones lying on the deck and threw it. It struck Olvir on the chest with such force that it not only knocked him unconscious, but also propelled him overboard into the sea. Somehow his men got him back on board, but for the time being, as the saga writer says, 'nobody knew whether he was alive or dead'. It was now the Hebrideans' turn to panic. Some of them cut the grappling ropes that they had attached to the earl's ship, and as the defenders rallied the remainder were soon driven from the deck. As Olvir's men began to row away their captain came to his senses and ordered them to stand fast, but by now no one was in the mood to listen to him. Olvir's flagship and six of the smaller vessels got away round Mull Head, and Paul pursued them southwards for what must have been nearly twenty miles, down the coast of South

Ronaldsay and into the Pentland Firth, before giving up the chase.
The other five Hebridean vessels had been abandoned in the bay at
Tankerness, and these the earl crewed with his own men.

With his original five longships, plus two more which came to
join him on the following day, Paul's fleet was now twelve strong.
He at once set sail for Shetland and arrived that night at Yell Sound,
between the islands of Yell and Mainland, where Rognvald's ships
still lay. It seems that the latter were beached and guarded only by a
small detachment while the rest of their crews were billeted inland,
because Paul quickly overwhelmed the guards, killed them and took
away the ships. Rashly Rognvald must have left his war chest on board,
because the saga says that Paul also acquired all his money, which he
kept for himself. The next morning a furious Rognvald brought his
Norwegian troops, reinforced by a large number of Shetland farmers,
down to the beach off which Paul's fleet lay. He challenged his rival
to come ashore and fight, to which Paul responded by inviting him to
go out and meet him at sea – which of course Rognvald could not do,
as all his ships were now in the hands of his enemy. Eventually Paul
returned to Orkney, leaving his rival stranded, and celebrated his
victory with a great feast. During the autumn Rognvald managed to
find passage back to Norway for himself and his men on a collection
of merchant ships. He had obviously been humiliated and the saga
writer says that people in Norway regarded his campaign as a joke,
although his father encouraged him to try again and began laying
plans for an expedition in the following spring.

The tables are turned

Paul was well aware that he would not be secure as long as his rival was
alive, and he ordered work to begin on a system of warning beacons
on outlying islands, so that he would receive warning if an enemy fleet
approached from Shetland. He also raised troops throughout Orkney

and kept them under arms until the beginning of winter, when he demobilised them on learning that Rognvald had returned to Norway. Meanwhile Olvir was still active, launching hit and run attacks at various points around the coast. In the course of one of these raids Olaf Hrolfsson of Gairsay, who had commanded one of Paul's ships at Tankerness, was trapped in a house and burned to death while visiting friends at Duncansby. Olaf's son was the notorious pirate Svein Asleifsson (Asleif was his mother), who would later exact his revenge by killing Olvir's grandmother Frakokk in a very similar hall-burning attack. Few of the participants at Tankerness were destined to die peacefully. That Christmas Svein Asleifsson got into a drunken quarrel with Svein 'Breast Rope', the hero of the battle, over a drinking game, the result of which was that the latter was fatally wounded with an axe blow to the head. Many people were apparently glad to see the back of Breast Rope, who had a reputation as a bully, but Svein Asleifsson fled to the Hebrides, and Earl Paul pronounced him an outlaw.

In the spring Kol and Rognvald put their plan into action. With the assistance of their friends, including King Harald, who provided a longship, they mustered a fleet of fourteen vessels in Shetland: six large longships, five smaller ones, and three cargo ships. On his father's advice Rognvald also made a bid for divine favour, promising to build a magnificent cathedral at Kirkwall in honour of his uncle, St Magnus, if he obtained the victory. Spies from Orkney had obviously revealed the existence of Paul's early warning system, and Kol then set out to neutralise it by a clever stratagem. He took a group of small vessels to within sight of Fair Isle, where the northernmost of Paul's beacons had been built, and raised their sails to half mast, while having the crews row in the opposite direction to the way the wind was blowing, so that although they appeared to be moving rapidly under sail they were in fact stationary. Then after a while he raised the sails fully, so that to an observer at a distance it would appear that they had

risen above the horizon and so must have moved closer. The idea was
that those manning the beacon on Fair Isle would mistake them for
a fleet of larger ships approaching fast from Shetland. The scheme
succeeded, and a Fair Isle farmer named Dagfinn Hlodvisson duly lit
the fire. His counterpart on North Ronaldsay, Thorstein Rognusson,
saw it and followed suit, and soon all the beacons through Orkney
were ablaze. Paul hastily mustered his army, but by this time Kol
was back in Shetland, and though the earl's men waited under arms
for three days, there was no sign of the enemy. Tempers were short,
and an argument broke out between Dagfinn and Thorstein, who
blamed the former for the false alarm, alleging that he had panicked
at the sight of a few fishermen. Eventually Thorstein seized an axe
and killed Dagfinn, at which a general brawl broke out. Paul restored
order only with difficulty, and had no choice but to send everyone
back to their homes.

Meanwhile one of Rognvald's agents, a Norwegian named Uni,
arrived on Fair Isle with three men in a six-oared fishing boat,
claiming to have been robbed by Rognvald and forced to flee from
Shetland. His story was so convincing that Dagfinn's successor, a man
named Eirik, befriended him and finally agreed to let him look after
the rebuilt warning beacon. Then the fleet set sail from Shetland,
carefully choosing a day when the combination of spring tides and
easterly winds would make the passage to Orkney easy from the north,
but would hamper Paul's movements between the islands. The Fair
Isle men once again went to light the beacon, but Uni had secretly
soaked it with water so that it would not burn. As soon as he realised
this Eirik sailed to Orkney to warn Earl Paul, but it was already too
late. Rognvald's fleet had landed on Westray, the northernmost of the
main Orkney islands, and forced the inhabitants into submission.
Paul was on Mainland, and the tide flowing through the Westray
Firth, together with the unfavourable wind, made it impossible for
his ships to reach his enemy. He therefore summoned a meeting of

his leading supporters to ask their advice, but their opinions varied widely. Some suggested buying Rognvald off, others recommended offering to share the earldom with him, while a minority wanted to fight, so that when the wind finally changed to north-westerly a brief window of opportunity for a counterattack on Westray had been wasted in inconclusive arguments. The outcome was that the bishop of Orkney was brought in to arrange a truce, but this did not stop the gradual defection of many of Paul's followers, with the result that he was forced to evacuate Mainland and set up his headquarters on the small island of Rousay.

At about this time Thorkel Flayer, another of the victors of Tankerness, was murdered, for reasons that the saga does not explain, by some of Svein Asleifsson's relatives. The killers then fled to join Rognvald, while Thorkel's son, Haflidi, naturally sought help from Paul. When Svein himself returned soon afterwards from the Hebrides, it was inevitable that he should gravitate towards his kinsmen in Rognvald's faction. But he went first to Atholl to visit Paul's sister Margaret, who was married to Earl Maddad. In Atholl they hatched a plot to replace Paul as earl of Orkney with Maddad and Margaret's son, Harald Maddadsson – a plot which could hardly have been hatched without the knowledge of the Scottish king, David I, bearing in mind the geographical proximity of Atholl to the centre of Scottish power as well as Maddad's royal connections. Then Svein set out for Orkney, sailing probably via the River Tay in a merchant ship with thirty men. This was an unusually large crew for a trading voyage, which suggests that Svein and his backers already had some violent plan in mind, and it is likely that they were already in communication with Rognvald, although the saga does not say so. As they were rowing past Rousay on their way to Svein's farm on the neighbouring island of Gairsay, they spotted some men on the shore. Svein ordered twenty of his own men to hide in their sleeping bags while the others rowed, so that their numbers would not be obvious and they would appear to be peaceable merchants. The ruse succeeded, and the watchers on shore shouted to them to take their cargo to Westness, on the south side of the island, where they could offer their goods for sale to the earl. Paul was on the shore hunting otters when Svein arrived, and the plotters were able to disembark and take the earl's party by surprise. In the ensuing fight six of Svein's men were killed along with nineteen of their opponents, but Paul himself was captured alive. Svein then made his escape back to Atholl with his prisoner. What happened to Paul after that is unclear. *Orkneyinga Saga* has an unlikely tale that he decided of his own free will to go into exile, but in order to discourage any attempts by his supporters to restore him he asked Svein to spread the rumour that he had been blinded and maimed. However, the saga writer adds that some believed that Paul really was imprisoned and blinded, and subsequently murdered, perhaps by Svein Aleifsson at the instigation of Margaret and Maddad. Blinding, castration or both were treatments commonly meted out to defeated rivals for power in early mediaeval Scotland, and we shall encounter several other examples in later chapters, but barbarous though this seems to a modern reader, we should not see it simply as a manifestation of primitive savagery. It was probably regarded as a way of removing a claimant and his posterity from consideration without going so far as to kill him, and as such it might be thought of as a sign of moderation compared, for example, to the 'blood eagling' of a renegade Norwegian prince (see Chapter 2), or the cold-blooded murder committed at Forfar in 1230 on the orders of a Christian king (Chapter 8).

Whatever the truth of the rumours concerning Earl Paul, Svein seems to have had some sort of leverage over earls Rognvald and Maddad, as well as David king of Scots. He certainly bore a charmed life afterwards, repeatedly avoiding punishment for his numerous crimes thanks to the favour and protection of these powerful men, until he was finally killed in a failed attack on Dublin sometime around 1170. In return Svein had enabled the victory of Rognvald Kali Kolsson, to whom he remained loyal for the rest of his life. Rognvald was obliged to share the earldom with the young Harald Maddadsson, but while he lived the former was the dominant partner, and a successful ruler of whom *Orkneyinga Saga* says that he was 'much loved in the isles and in many other places too'. In 1137 he began the building of St Magnus's Cathedral, and in 1151, like Thorfinn the Mighty, he undertook a celebrated pilgrimage, this time as far as the Holy Land. In 1192 Rognvald himself was canonised by Pope Celestine III. After his death in a skirmish with rebels in 1158 Harald took over as sole earl, but if the Scottish kings imagined that they had managed to install a compliant puppet in Orkney, they were soon to learn otherwise.

Tankerness today

Nowadays Tankerness (grid reference HY510084) is a very quiet hamlet on the western shore of Deer Sound, about five miles east of Kirkwall. There is an occasional bus, but the site is only two miles from Kirkwall Airport, which has much more frequent access by public transport. There is nothing at Tankerness to indicate the battle site (the memorial at Mull of Deerness, just outside the bay, commemorates 200 Covenanter prisoners who were drowned in a shipwreck in 1679), but the beach at Mill Sand is a pleasant place to visit, full of hares and bird life, and with good views across the sound towards Mull Head. The beach is still littered with large stones of the sort which were collected for use as missiles in the battle. St Magnus's Cathedral in Kirkwall remains as a monument to Rognvald's victory and his vision.

Chapter 5

The Rise, Fall and Legacy of Somerled the Great: Renfrew, 1164

Date: 1164

Location: Braehead, near Renfrew, Renfrewshire

Combatants: Islemen and Irish under Somerled of Argyll versus local Scottish militia led by Bishop Herbert of Glasgow

Outcome: Scottish victory

Perhaps Dorrud's witches really could foretell the future, because the most renowned of all the contenders for leadership in the mediaeval Highlands and Islands in the two centuries after the Battle of Clontarf did come from the 'outer headlands'. By the twelfth century the earldom of Orkney had a counterpart in the west in the Kingdom of the Isles. This extended over most of the offshore islands on the west coast of Scotland plus the Isle of Man, from which it took its alternative name of the Kingdom of Man or Mann. Like the earldom it had its origins in the ninth century, when the first recorded Viking incursions into the Hebrides took place, though here the Scandinavian influence on the earlier Celtic culture was less overwhelming. As early as 802 we hear of Viking raids on the sacred island of Iona, the home of St Columba and burial place of the Scottish kings, and by 849 these had become so intolerable that the monks of Iona evacuated the place, taking with them the precious relics of Columba. Until the early ninth century the islands south of the Ardnamurchan Peninsula had belonged to the kingdom of Dal Riata, but by the 860s they had already been lost to the Scandinavian invaders. The Irish *Annals of the Four Masters* mention under the year 853 the death of Gofraidh mac Fearghus, an ally of the Scottish king Kenneth MacAlpin, who is described as 'toiseach Innsi Gall' or 'chief of the Isles'. Presumably he held the Hebrides as Kenneth's appointee or vassal, but we are not told how he died, and after him there seems to have been a political vacuum in which the Norse raiders flourished unmolested. In 871 they sacked Dumbarton Castle on the River Clyde, then the capital of the British kingdom of Alt Clut or Strathclyde, and either carried away its leading citizens to Ireland or forced them into exile. As they had done in Fortriu a generation earlier, the Vikings were unwittingly strengthening the hand of the new Scottish monarchy by weakening its rivals on the mainland.

The Kingdom of the Isles

As discussed in Chapter 2, the Norwegian king Harald Fairhair brought Orkney and Shetland at least nominally under his authority in 875, and soon afterwards, according to *Orkneyinga Saga,* he sent an expedition to subdue the pirates who were also infesting the Hebrides. Both *Laxdaela Saga* and *Eyrbyggja Saga* identify the leader of this expedition as Ketill Bjornsson, known as Ketill Flatnose, who was himself a notorious pirate. Ketill carried out his mission successfully, but then refused to pay tribute to Harald, and instead proclaimed himself an independent ruler of what he called the Kingdom of the Sudreyar, or 'Southern Isles'. Harald confiscated Ketill's estates in Norway, but was unable to threaten his authority in the Isles, which remained de facto independent. The subsequent history of the region is poorly documented, but by about 900 the Isle of Man had been added to the realm. This island, which to judge from the scanty records in the Annals of Ulster and elsewhere had until then been sporadically occupied by various Irish and English rulers, was richer and more fertile than the Hebrides, as well as being further removed from any threat from Norway, and soon became the kingdom's main centre of power.

By 989 the *Annals of Ulster* were using the term '*Ri Inse Gall*', or 'King of the Isles', to refer to a certain Gofraid mac Arailt, which is clearly a Gaelic form of the Norse name Godfred Haraldsson. *Orkneyinga Saga* says that the Hebrides were temporarily subject to the great Orkney earls Sigurd the Stout and Thorfinn the Mighty, but although they levied troops or hired mercenaries there the precise nature of the control they exercised is not explained. It was not until the reign of King Magnus 'Berfoettr', or 'Barelegs', of Norway in the 1090s that they were actually brought under Norwegian control. In 1098 Magnus brought a large fleet to Orkney, where he deposed earls Erlend and Paul and installed his own son, Sigurd Magnusson. He went on to ravage the Hebrides, conquer the Isle of Man and raid as far south as Anglesey. William of Malmesbury thought that his intention was to conquer England, but in fact he went no further than North Wales before turning back. He did, however, capture the then '*Ri Inse Gall*', Logmadr, and proclaim Norwegian sovereignty over the Hebrides and Man. He then signed a treaty with King Edgar of Scotland, who formally recognised his claim to 'the Isles'. At this time the term seems to have included not only the Inner and Outer Hebrides and the Isle of Man, but the Scottish mainland peninsulas of Kintyre, Morvern and Ardnamurchan, all of which were more easily accessible by sea than by land. According to *Heimskringla*, Magnus had insisted that the Scots recognise his right to every island around which a ship could sail, and then had his longships dragged across the two-mile-wide isthmus at Tarbert in order to establish his claim to Kintyre. In fact, given the Norwegian dominance at sea, none of the peninsulas in question could have been controlled effectively by the Scots in any case. Magnus died only five years after the treaty was signed, however, and the region soon reverted to its accustomed independence. The local rulers in the Isles might even have been obliged to accept some sort of tributary relationship with the king of Scots, because David I's army at the Battle of Standard in 1138 included a contingent of Islemen, though it is not clear whether these were mercenaries, volunteers, or serving under similar terms to the men levied from Scotland itself. Certainly the kings of Norway retained at least nominal authority over the region, because in 1152 Godred, the son of King Olaf of Man, was in their country to do homage to King Inge, probably on behalf of his ageing father. But by this time new powers were emerging in the Hebrides.

The Rise of Somerled

Somerled first appears in the historical record in the year 1153, when following the death of David I he 'rose in rebellion', as the pro-Scottish *Holyrood Chronicle* puts it, against David's successor Malcolm IV. Of his ancestry and earlier life nothing definite is known from contemporary sources. In later centuries numerous family trees were published purporting to trace his ancestry back to legendary figures of Scottish or Irish history, and in turn linking him to the clans which claimed him as an ancestor, but these often contradict each other and none can be regarded as authoritative. Recent DNA studies have, however, suggested that these traditional claims of descent from Somerled may have a basis in fact. A large proportion of men with the names MacDonald, MacAlister and MacDougall have been found to carry genetic markers which suggest a common descent from a male ancestor who may have lived around the twelfth century (Moffat & Wilson, 2011), leading to the suggestion that Somerled might have as many as 500,000 living descendants in the twenty-first century. Furthermore, this particular marker is rare elsewhere in Gaelic-speaking Scotland, but very common in Norway. Somerled's name is in fact of Scandinavian origin, deriving from the Norse Sumarlidi or 'Summer Raider', but his father's name, known from his Gaelic appellation Somairle mac Gillebrichte ('son of the servant of Saint Bridget'), is just as obviously Celtic. So all we can say for certain is that his background was in the mixed Norse-Celtic culture typical of the Isles at that time, and that he was probably from a prominent local family.

Somerled's career is mentioned in four roughly contemporary writings: the *Chronicle of Man*, the Holyrood and Melrose chronicles, and the *Carmen de Morte Sumerledi*, or 'Song of the Death of Somerled'. The latter work is a short poem written in Latin by a certain William, a clerk of Glasgow, who claims to have been an eyewitness of the Battle of Renfrew. It is therefore likely that it dates from not long after the events in question, although its reliability has been questioned, and contrary to what the title might lead us to expect it is strongly biased against Somerled, whom William, like the Holyrood chronicler, regarded as a traitor to the King of Scots. An opposing point of view, and a great deal more detail about his life, is provided by several histories of Clan Donald, of which Somerled was traditionally regarded as the founder. These include the English language *History of the MacDonalds* by Hugh MacDonald of Sleat, and the Gaelic 'Red' and 'Black' Books of Clanranald, all of which were written in the late seventeenth century. These have often been dismissed as unreliable because of their late date, but Marsden (2000) has convincingly argued that in view of the careful attention given to the accurate oral transmission of genealogical information in Gaelic culture, and the undoubted importance of Somerled in the history of the clan, they should not be disregarded as sources of original material, however historically questionable some of the details may be.

According to this MacDonald tradition, by the time of Somerled's birth – which must have been not long after 1100 – his family had fallen on hard times. His grandfather Gilledomnan had lost his lands and become a refugee in Ireland some time towards the end of the eleventh century – possibly, as Marsden speculates, as a result of the campaigns of Magnus Barelegs, whom the Norse poets described as the 'expeller of the Scots' from the Hebrides. Gillebrichte, Somerled's father, returned to the Isles with a small band of followers and lived for some years as an outlaw, launching attacks on the Norsemen when opportunity offered and taking refuge in the mountains, hence his nickname '*na h-Uamh*', or 'Gillebrichte of the cave'. The MacDonald histories give differing versions of what happened next, but Gillebrichte and his son Somerled were either attacked by a Viking army, or answered a call by the Gaelic people of Morvern to liberate them from the Scandinavians who had occupied their lands. Morvern is a peninsula lying to the south of Ardnamurchan, which as discussed above was technically regarded as one of the 'isles' claimed by the kings of Norway. According to Hugh MacDonald of Sleat, however, it was occupied by the ancestors of the Gaelic clans of MacInnes and MacGilvray. In fact any reference to modern clans in this era must surely be anachronistic, and modern scholars doubt that there would have been such a clear distinction between Gaels and Norse after more than three centuries of cultural mixing along the west Scottish coast. But there may well have been some more recent Scandinavian settlers, perhaps brought over by King Magnus, whose presence was resented by the more established residents, and we are told that the locals were planning an uprising but could find no one to lead them. At this point Somerled, who had now come of age and was looking to make a name for himself, arrived fortuitously in Morvern 'with his bow, quiver and sword', and was immediately acclaimed as their leader. The date of this occurrence – if indeed it is historical – is not certain, but Somerled had a grown-up son by 1154, so the campaign must have occurred at least twenty years earlier. Battle was joined somewhere on the coast of Morvern.

John Marsden doubts all of these stories, but if there is any truth in them they provide some interesting evidence for Somerled's military abilities, because he is said to have come up with a clever plan to persuade the enemy that his troops were more numerous than they actually were. Three times they marched around a hill and appeared wearing different clothing – either coats, shirts and full armour, or according to another version showing both sides of cowhides prepared for the occasion – in order to give the impression of three different units. Seeing that some of the Vikings were still on board their ships, Somerled then gave the order to attack, saying that the enemy on the shore 'would fight but faintly so near to their ships', perhaps because they believed that retreat would be easy, or possibly because they would resent the fact that their comrades on the ships were not sharing the danger. Hugh says that Somerled intensified the psychological warfare by ripping out the heart of the first man he killed and ordering his followers to do the same. This he justified on the grounds (surely incorrect by this date) that the Norsemen were not Christians, but this deliberate mutilation itself sounds like a pagan custom rather than a Christian one. Nevertheless the Vikings, believing that they were being attacked by overwhelming numbers, and perhaps shocked by the ferocity of the onslaught, panicked and fled. Three of their leaders were killed in the rout, and many others drowned trying to reach the ships. A later oral tradition suggests that there was an extended pursuit, with the defeated Norsemen escaping northwards across Loch Sunart and one of their chiefs, Torquil, being overtaken while crossing a ford at Acharacle, three miles inland from the loch. This may, however, be a later attempt to explain the name, which was said to derive from the Gaelic Ath Tharacaill, 'Torquil's Ford', but could equally well be Achadh Tharacaill or 'Torquil's Field', a name with altogether more peaceful connotations.

Bishop Wimund

A story told by the English chronicler William of Newburgh sheds some interesting light on conditions in the Isles around this time. An Englishman of obscure origins named Wimund, who had been educated at Furness Abbey in Cumbria, was sent to help set up a new foundation on the Isle of Man. King Olaf of Man had apparently granted to the monks of the abbey the right to elect the Bishop of the Isles, and at some point before 1140 Wimund, despite his youth and inexperience, was selected for the position and took up his seat at Snizort on the Isle of Skye, which was then part of the Kingdom of Man. This, however, did not satisfy his ambition, so he announced that he was actually the son of the Earl of Moray, and had been deprived of his rightful inheritance by King David of Scotland. Aided by what William of Newburgh describes as his charismatic personality, as well as, no doubt, by the promise of plunder, he collected a band of desperate adventurers and began to launch attacks on the Scottish mainland. We are not told that Olaf made any attempt to bring him under control, which suggests that his authority over Skye was little more than nominal. David tried repeatedly to bring Wimund to battle, but he carefully avoided the royal forces and retreated to the Isles whenever he was hard pressed, so that eventually the king gave up and granted him lands around Furness in exchange for peace. However, Wimund's behaviour became more and more tyrannical, until finally his followers turned against him, blinded and castrated him and drove him into exile. He spent the rest of his life at Byland Abbey in Yorkshire, where William of Newburgh met and spoke to him. Wimund remained unrepentant, assuring William that if he 'had only the eye of a sparrow' he would make his enemies regret what they had done to him. Although something of a sideshow compared to the great events of the time, Wimund's career suggests something of the lawless conditions which must have prevailed in the Isles during

Somerled's early years. What we know of him is due only to a chance meeting with an English chronicler, so it is likely that there were many other similar warlords whose activities have not been recorded.

War with the Kingdom of Man and the 'Epiphany Battle'

In the aftermath of his victory in Morvern Somerled became ruler not only of that peninsula, but also of the coastal districts to the south: Lorn, Argyll, Knapdale and Kintyre, which he held until his death. His father disappears from the record at this point, although the date and circumstances of his death are not known. Neither do we have any details of Somerled's own career over the next two decades, though according to *Orkneyinga Saga* he married Ragnhild, a daughter of King Olaf of Man, by whom he had three sons: Dugall, Ranald and Angus. It is an intriguing possibility that he may have been one of the leaders of the Islemen who fought in the army of King David against the English at the Battle of the Standard in 1138; if so he must somehow have escaped from the disaster not only with his life, but also with his reputation and most of his following intact, because when he reappears fifteen years after the battle, it is as one of the leading magnates in the land.

David I died in May 1153 after a successful reign of twenty-nine years, and was succeeded by his twelve-year-old grandson Malcolm IV, his only son Prince Henry having died the year before. Not surprisingly the transition was marked by what the *Holyrood Chronicle* describes as 'grievous disturbances over the greater part of Scotland', the worst of which were ascribed to 'Somerled and his nephews, that is to say the sons of Malcolm'. This Malcolm has generally been identified with Malcolm MacHeth, a rival claimant to the Scottish throne whose career is discussed in Chapter 6. The implication of the chronicle's statement about his nephews ('nepotes' in Latin) is of course that Somerled and Malcolm were related, but exactly how is unclear. The latter may have been married to a sister, or possibly a daughter, of Somerled, though as this would presumably have happened before Malcolm was captured and imprisoned by David in 1134, it seems unlikely that Somerled would have had a daughter of marriageable age at that time. In any case this emphasises how Somerled had already been accepted as an equal by the leading families of the west. Malcolm was apparently still in custody in Roxburgh Castle at the time of the 1153 revolt, and one of its objectives may have been to obtain his release, which did in fact take place four years later. Apart from this we know nothing for certain of the course of the rebellion, though the wording of the chronicle implies that Somerled was its leader. The *Carmen de Morte Sumerledi* accuses him of having once sacked Glasgow, which was already a wealthy port and the site of a bishopric, and where 'gardens, fields and plough lands' were laid waste, and the people forced to flee from 'the blows of two-edged swords'. However the source does not put a date on this event, so it may have happened either during the course of this war, or possibly in the Renfrew campaign of 1164. The seventeenth-century history of Hugh MacDonald says that the Scottish nobility envied Somerled 'for his fortune and valour', and so they sent an army under the command of Gilchrist, the Thane of Angus, to crush him. The invaders ravaged Argyll until Somerled and his vassals caught up with them at an unknown location, and a bloody battle was fought in which Somerled lost 2,000 men and his opponent no fewer than 7,000. Despite the slaughter no decision had been reached by nightfall, and on the following morning both armies retreated. Marsden points out that this story is not corroborated by any contemporary source, and bears suspicious similarities to other probably fictional battles described in the MacDonald histories. However Professor R.A. MacDonald (1998) has provisionally identified Gilchrist with a documented person of that name, the Earl of Menteith, who was active in the following decade. As Menteith, unlike Angus, has a border with

Argyll, he would have been a plausible choice to lead an invasion, and the mention of Angus might be an understandable mistake by the MacDonald chronicler writing nearly five centuries later.

Whether this war was a real event or not, Somerled was about to be drawn into an even more serious conflict on his southern front. Little more than a month after the death of King David, Olaf of Man was murdered by three of his nephews who had returned from exile in Dublin, and the Kingdom of Man was plunged, like Scotland, into civil war. Olaf's son Godred, known as 'the Black', who was in Norway at the time, returned in 1154 and was accepted as the rightful king by the chiefs of the Isles, among whom was presumably his brother-in-law, Somerled. With their support Godred landed on the Isle of Man and captured the assassins, who were put to death or blinded. According to the *Chronicle of Man* he went on to campaign unsuccessfully in Ireland, but on his return he sent home the military contingents of the chiefs, and once they were powerless to defend themselves he began to behave tyrannically towards them, disinheriting some and depriving others of various dignities. One of the most powerful of them, Thorfinn son of Ottar, then approached Somerled and suggested that they should put forward the latter's eldest son Dugall, who had a claim to the kingship through his mother, as a rival candidate. Dugall set out on a journey through the Isles to gather support, but was betrayed by a chief named Paul who sent a message to Godred warning him of the plot. Godred immediately assembled a fleet and set sail from Man, while Somerled moved to intercept him with a force which the *Chronicle of Man* says comprised eighty ships. The two fleets met, according to the *Chronicle*, 'in the year 1156 on the night of the Lord's Epiphany', or in other words on the night of the 5 to 6 January. The location of the battle is not given in any early source, but most recent authors have followed a MacDonald tradition, first recorded in 1896, that places it off the coast of Islay (Marsden). Wallace Clark (1993), who actually sailed a replica mediaeval galley through the Isles in the early 1990s, considered that the west coast of that island would have been far too exposed for ships to operate in winter, and that the most likely site for the battle is the Sound of Islay, a narrow channel between the islands of Islay and Jura, which offered a well-used shipping route sheltered from the prevailing west winds.

That fleets could sail at all off the west coast of Scotland in the depths of winter may seem surprising, but these sailors were heirs to the Norse tradition of seafaring, with long experience of surviving bad weather. For example, *Orkneyinga Saga* tells us that ships regularly navigated the even more dangerous waters of the Pentland Firth at the Christmas season. Clark also points out that the Irish *Annals of the Four Masters* describe 'great snow and intense frost' during this winter, and that such conditions often produce cold but calm weather at sea. Epiphany would have been about a week before the full moon, which would also have been an aid to navigation and fighting at night, but Clark argues that the battle could actually have taken place up to six days after the feast, which would still have been the closest point of reference for the chroniclers. We can therefore imagine the fleets approaching each other under oars by the light of the moon, perhaps with additional illumination provided by reflection from snow-covered hills on either side of the strait, which at its narrowest is less than a mile wide. The *Chronicle of Man* gives no details of the course of the fighting, but tells of 'great slaughter of men on either side'. Probably it took the form of a massive boarding fight like Tankerness, but in this case no one who fell into the freezing sea in the darkness is likely to have survived.

Naval warfare in the Hebrides

The only other Hebridean sea battle of the Middle Ages whose course is known in any detail is Bloody Bay, which took place around 1484 (Rixson). The traditional accounts, derived mainly from the oral traditions of Clan MacLean, differ in detail but give us a few interesting hints on naval tactics, which are unlikely to have evolved much in the three centuries since the Epiphany Battle. Bloody Bay, which was situated somewhere off the south coast of the Ardnamurchan Peninsula, was the scene of a clash between the fleets of one of Somerled's descendants, John MacDonald, Lord of the Isles, and his rebellious son Angus Og. Angus's four galleys were sailing east towards Loch Sunart when they spotted a vessel flying what they thought was the flag of their enemies, the MacLeans. They went in pursuit, only to discover that it actually belonged to someone else, but by this time at least five galleys belonging to chiefs loyal to John had spotted them and come out to head them off. Eventually, after a fierce fight, Angus was victorious. One of the opposing captains was mortally wounded by two arrows, and his ship was then boarded and taken. The galley of MacLeod of Harris was also grappled and boarded after one of Angus's men had jammed its rudder by shoving an oar between it and the stern post – though Wallace Clark points out that jamming the rudder would not prevented the ship from manoeuvring if it was under oars, which it surely must have been. MacNeil of Barra was last seen fleeing for the open sea with three enemy vessels in pursuit, while the other survivors of the defeated fleet took refuge in Tobermory harbour on the nearby island of Mull.

Among the things that this account tells us is that tactics included both long-range archery and boarding fights, still very much in the style of the encounters described in the Viking sagas. One decree of the late sixteenth century quoted by Rixson states that only 'gentlemen' were allowed to go to sea, and that the labouring classes were forbidden to join them, probably for fear that agriculture would be neglected in favour of piracy. However, even if this was true in Somerled's day, it does not mean that every crewman would have been fully equipped with expensive mail armour; the same source says that even at that late date, of the 6,000 men who could be raised for naval service in the Hebrides, only 2,000 had the full panoply of aketon, mail and helmet. Most of the rest would probably have been archers, whose ability to strike at long range was especially valuable during the long pre-battle phase when the fleets were labouring towards each other under oars. Along with the steering oar, Somerled is also sometimes credited with the introduction of fighting tops on the masts, from which archers could shoot down onto the enemy's decks (Clark), but the evidence for this is tenuous. What might be a fighting top is depicted on the Great Seals of Alexander of Lorn and Angus Mor of Islay (Rixson), but these date from no earlier than 1292. A fifteenth-century description of the now lost seal of Somerled's son Ranald describes a device of 'a ship full of armed men', and it seems to be on this basis that Clark assumes that Somerled's own seal was identical to the late thirteenth-century version. In fact fighting tops of this type are not depicted elsewhere in art, which suggests that if they had ever been in use in the Isles they had not been very successful. Certainly there is no reason to follow Clark in speculating that they might have been a decisive factor in Somerled's victory in the Epiphany Battle.

Modern writers are almost unanimous that ramming tactics were not used in Hebridean galley fights, though Clark does discuss this possibility, concluding that the smaller Hebridean birlinns were more solidly built than the larger Viking longships, and so their bows would have been better able to withstand the impact if they had been employed in this way. It would also have been a logical way to exploit the superior manoeuvrability of the smaller galleys, which were known to be vulnerable in a traditional boarding fight. If striking the side of an enemy galley at a speed of three knots or more, he says, an attacker's bow could break the gunwale and perhaps some of the strakes as far as the waterline, and either let in water by that means or heel the victim over until it filled with water and had to be abandoned. It would not then sink, but would float waterlogged and could perhaps be recovered later. Oars would also of course be vulnerable to a ramming attack. Ramming seems not to be described in any actual battle, but detailed accounts of sea fights are so rare that this negative evidence cannot be regarded as conclusive. In fact a story related by Matheson (2014) does suggest that enemy ships could have been sunk by such methods, and that captains were apparently aware of the possibility. Sometime in the thirteenth century the chief of the Nicholsons, a family of Norse descent based in Lewis and in Assynt in Sutherland, married his daughter to Murdoch, a younger son of the MacLeods of Harris. One day the chief set out to cross the Minch to visit his relatives, taking his wife and their other children with him. Murdoch sailed out from Harris with his wife to meet them and escort them home, but temporarily lost his bearings in a patch of mist, and when it cleared he found his birlinn on a collision course with the side of the other vessel. There was still just time to alter course, but Murdoch's wife urged him not to do so, pointing out that the family in front of them were all that stood between her own son and the inheritance of vast estates in Lewis. So Murdoch held his course and struck the Nicholson boat amidships, sinking it and leaving his in-laws to drown. We can also deduce from the events at Bloody Bay that flags or banners were flown at sea as a means of identification, and perhaps also for signalling. Exactly what designs were used at this period is not known, though they probably bore little resemblance to the heraldic clan banners seen today.

The partition of the Isles

When day dawned over the Sound of Islay the issue was still in the balance, so Somerled and Godred opened negotiations. We do not know the details of their discussions, but the eventual outcome was that the kingdom was partitioned. The *Chronicle of Man* describes this battle as 'the cause of the ruin of the Kingdom of the Isles', but does not state exactly how it was divided. It seems, however, that Godred retained the Isle of Man and the Hebrides north of Ardnamurchan, while Somerled's portion comprised the more southerly islands of the Scottish coast, including Islay and Mull, plus the peninsula of Kintyre. From a strategic point of view, therefore, the islands which Godred ceded drove a wedge between the two widely separated remaining parts of his kingdom, which must have made communication very difficult. Not surprisingly, this was not the end of the conflict. Two years later, according to the *Chronicle of Man*, Somerled attacked the Isle of Man with a fleet of fifty-three ships and this time decisively defeated his rival; though whether this was another battle fought at sea, or whether it took place on the island itself, the chronicle does not tell us. After his victory Somerled 'devastated the whole island', while Godred fled to Norway to ask the king there for help. This might suggest that Somerled actually occupied Man for a time, but we are not specifically told this. The same source says that Godred returned with a Norwegian army in 1164, but by that time Somerled was either dead or at least deeply involved in the campaign which was to end in his death, and the two deadly rivals never again met in battle. Instead Godred had to deal with a revolt by his own brother, which he brutally suppressed. He resumed his rule over Man and remained on the throne until 1187, but he never regained the islands which he had lost in 1156.

Our sources are mostly silent regarding Somerled's activities in the six years between his attack on Man and the Battle of Renfrew. The *Melrose Chronicle* says that by 1164 he had been in rebellion against King Malcolm for twelve years, meaning presumably since the events following Malcolm's accession in 1153, but in fact there is good reason to believe that at some point during this period he had become reconciled with the king. Malcolm was facing serious problems elsewhere at this time. In 1157 Somerled's presumed brother-in-law Malcolm MacHeth had been released from prison, thus removing one obvious cause of disagreement, but in the same year Henry II of England had bullied the king of Scots into accepting vassal status and surrendering Northumberland and Cumbria, which had come under Scottish control during the chaotic reign of King Stephen in England. Two years later Malcolm travelled to join Henry in France, where he was knighted by his new overlord. This might have seemed to the young Scottish monarch a desirable sign of acceptance into the mainstream feudal society of Europe, but to his own nobles it looked more like a national humiliation. On his return Malcolm foiled a plot by six Scottish earls to take him prisoner at Perth, and he also had to take an army into Galloway on three occasions to suppress rebellion there. He was therefore, no doubt, eager to make peace with Somerled in order to secure his western frontier, and such an agreement is alluded to by a charter, ascribed by Professor Barrow to 1160, which is dated 'at Perth on the Christmas following the agreement between the king and Somerled'. That the two men actually met in person on at least one occasion is also suggested by the nickname of 'Sit by the King' which William of Glasgow ascribes to Somerled.

The Renfrew campaign

The battle at Renfrew is relatively well documented by the standards of the time. The conflict was obviously recognised then as being of significance as far afield as England and Ireland, and is also mentioned in the *Chronica* of Roger of Howden, the Irish *Annals of Tigernach* and *Annals of Ulster*, the *Chronicle of Man*, the Scottish *Gesta Annalia*, the chronicles of Melrose and Holyrood, and Walter Bower's fifteenth-century *Scotichronicon*. What we do not know is what motivated Somerled to launch his attack on the Scottish mainland and challenge directly the growing power of the monarch with whom he had just become reconciled. Hugh MacDonald suggests that the jealousy which had induced the nobles at the king's court to dispatch Earl Gilchrist against Somerled was still a factor, and that when he realised this he decided on a pre-emptive strike, resolving 'to lose all, or possess all he had in the Highlands'. Hugh also says that while King Malcolm acknowledged Somerled's right to the Isles proper, he had demanded the restoration of 'Argyll and Kintyre', or in other words those peninsulas which Magnus Barelegs had managed to include in the territories ceded to him in 1098. The *Holyrood Chronicle* is less charitable to Somerled, stating that he attacked the mainland purely for plunder, while the *Chronicle of Man* ascribes to him 'the intention of subduing the whole of Scotland', which can hardly have been a realistic goal. Professor MacDonald (1998) has pointed out that Somerled's main target seems to have been the lands around Renfrew which formed the power base of Walter fitz Alan, Steward of Scotland and head of the family which later became known as the Stewarts. This family, like the Bruces, had spearheaded King David's policy of feudalisation and been rewarded with extensive holdings which would eventually enable them to make their own bid for the throne. Possibly Walter's presence on the west coast made him a more immediate threat to Somerled than the king himself, especially if he suspected – rightly or wrongly – that he might be induced to follow Gilchrist's example and lead an army against the Isles.

Whatever his reasons, Somerled's campaign was mounted with all the resources he could muster. According to the Irish sources he drew his forces from as far away as Dublin as well as from Argyll, Kintyre and the Isles. The *Melrose Chronicle* also mentions Irish troops. Those from the Scottish mainland and the Isles were presumably levied directly by Somerled as their overlord, but it is not clear how the Irish were recruited – perhaps as individual mercenaries, or more likely supplied through an alliance with the city of Dublin or the king of Leinster, Diarmait mac Murchada. The *Chronicle of Man* tells us that they sailed in 160 ships, which should give us an idea of the overall size of the army. Unfortunately we do not know how many men each ship carried, and they probably varied greatly in size (see Chapter

1). Reckoning a generous forty per ship would give us approximately 6,400 men. This ties in fairly well with the 6,000 that the sixteenth-century source mentioned above suggests for the armed strength of the Hebrides; Somerled did not control all of the Hebrides, but he also had an unknown number of Irish troops to compensate. According to Hugh MacDonald he first landed at Greenock, where he conducted fruitless negotiations with King Malcolm, then moved twelve miles eastwards up the estuary of the River Clyde to Renfrew, where he was brought to battle. Thomas Pennant, in his *Tour in Scotland and Voyage to the Hebrides* of 1774, refers to a 'mount or tumulus' on a hill known as The Knock, on the road between Renfrew and Paisley, with a standing stone on the top. 'Near this place', he says, 'was defeated and slain Sumerled, Thane of Argyll', and he goes on to suggest that it is 'not improbable' that the monument had been raised in his memory. In fact there are several earlier accounts of this stone, which was demolished not long after Pennant wrote, which refer to it as 'Queen Blearie's Stone' and link it to the death of Marjorie Bruce, daughter of King Robert, in 1317. The site is about two miles inland, north-east of the centre of Paisley, and apart from this rather speculative account there seems to be nothing to link it to Somerled. Probably the origin of the fourteenth-century monument had been largely forgotten locally, and Pennant's informants had confused it with the twelfth-century battle which was known to have been fought somewhere in the general area. William of Glasgow's account implies that the encounter took place much nearer to the place where Somerled's ships were moored on the south bank of the Clyde. The most likely location would therefore be east of the modern centre of Renfrew, where the Braehead shopping complex now stands beside the river. The invaders disembarked from their galleys somewhere along this shore and must have been preparing to march inland, but it seems that a scratch force of local levies had been assembled to meet them.

The *Carmen* is the only truly contemporary account of this battle, and its author implies that he was present himself and actually witnessed at least some of the events he narrates: 'that which he saw and heard, William has composed'. The author was clearly horrified by the behaviour of the Islemen, whose 'barbarous hands' inflicted untold cruelties on the peaceful local people, and whose leader, he insists, was not only 'the cruellest of foes' but also 'foul with treachery'. He gives few details of the actual fighting, but clearly implies that Somerled was defeated by a numerically smaller but far more effective opponent: the *Carmen* speaks of the 'destruction of the treacherous thousands' (in other words the Islemen), but claims that 'not one of those who fought them was wounded here or died'. It is hard to believe that there were no casualties at all among the victors, but the *Annals of Ulster* list the dead as 'men of Argyll and of Kintyre... men of the Hebrides, and foreigners of Dublin', all of whom must have been serving with Somerled. According to the *Carmen*, Somerled's head was cut off and later presented to Herbert, the bishop of Glasgow, which suggests that Herbert may have been in command of the Scottish forces. Walter fitz Alan controlled Renfrew at the time and so is often credited with the victory, but none of our sources actually state that he was present. We need not assume that because the men were recruited locally they were lacking in military skill or experience, and if they included a contingent from Glasgow, as seems likely, they would have had a strong motive for revenge after Somerled's earlier devastating attack on their city. Certainly in the early thirteenth century the people of Glasgow already had a reputation as very tough customers. In 1235, according to the *Melrose Chronicle*, a band of Irish soldiers of fortune was unwise enough to approach the town, and when their presence was discovered the citizens went out and slaughtered them. From the ferocity of the Glaswegians' response it seems that they remembered all too well the treatment they had once received from Somerled's Islemen and Irish allies:

the lucky ones were decapitated, but two of their leaders were taken prisoner and later torn to pieces by horses. It was also predominantly a scratch force of local levies from this part of Scotland that fought the Norwegians to a stalemate at the Battle of Largs (see Chapter 8).

The apparently one-sided nature of the combat has led some commentators to suppose that it involved heavily armoured mounted knights on the Anglo-Norman model riding down an ill-equipped rabble. We know that Norman knights were capable of routing much larger infantry forces by a swift and ruthless attack. For example, Matthew Paris relates how Roger de Quincy, Constable of Scotland, escaped from a siege in Galloway in 1247 by charging the enemy on horseback single-handed: 'they fell to either side of him; and so he cleft and scattered the whole army' (Strickland, in Spiers, ed, 2012). Somerled, recklessly exposed in the front of his army in the heroic Norse-Celtic tradition, might then have been ridden down by an unexpected mounted charge, knocked down by a lance thrust and quickly decapitated before his followers could react. Two principal objections have been raised to this scenario. One is that Scottish armies of the time appear not to have deployed large numbers of such knights. David I had attempted to increase the number of such troops available to the crown by extending the feudal system into those regions of Scotland which he controlled, but Professor Barrow has estimated that even in the late twelfth century there were only around a hundred knights' fees in the whole of the country. In that case many of the 200 knights whom John of Worcester says were in the Scottish army at the Battle of the Standard in 1138 must have been mercenaries, and this number presumably represents the maximum available to a national army, commanded by the king himself, for a major campaign in England. How many knights might have been raised at short notice by a local magnate to confront Somerled at Renfrew we can only guess, but it must have been considerably fewer than a hundred. Walter fitz Alan, if he was present, might have commanded a number of feudal vassals equipped as knights, but it is not clear what sort of men would have been available to Bishop Herbert.

The second objection is based on evidence that at least some Highlands and Islands forces were by no means unduly vulnerable to the close-order mounted charge with lance and sword on which the Normans relied. The Welsh chronicler Gerald de Barri describes the 'men of the Hebrides' who fought at Dublin in 1171 as fighting with long-handled axes. In other words they were similarly armed to the English huscarles of King Harold Godwinsson who had given the Norman cavalry so much trouble a century before at Hastings, and to the gallowglasses who led resistance to the English in Ireland until the sixteenth century. Admittedly some writers did not believe that such troops were particularly effective against cavalry: Barnaby Rich, writing in *A New Description of Ireland* (1610), describes the gallowglasses at the Battle of Monasternenagh (1579) as 'neither good against horsemen, nor able to endure an encounter with pikes'. However, this is a very late reference, from a time when the gallowglass tradition might have been in decline, and the plate-armoured cavalry and 18ft pikes of the sixteenth century would have been a very different proposition from anything to be found in the twelfth. By contrast John Barbour, in *The Bruce*, describes how at the Battle of Dalrigh in 1306 Robert the Bruce's MacDougall opponents 'fought so fiercely with axes (for they were each and all on foot) that they slew many of Bruce's horse, or gave great wounds to some,' forcing the king's men to retreat for fear of losing all their mounts. It should also be borne in mind that Highland contingents seem to have punched well above their weight in a number of clashes with English armies. At Bannockburn, for example, Somerled's descendants the MacDonalds earned by their valour the prestigious place on the right flank of any army in which they subsequently served. And at Flodden in 1513, the Highlanders under the Earl of Huntly 'with their bows and twa handit swords' (Pitscottie, quoted in Cannan, 2009) were the only division to achieve any success on what was otherwise a disastrous day for the Scots.

A more plausible reconstruction of the battle at Renfrew can in any case be attempted on the basis of what William of Glasgow actually says. Although there were only a hundred defenders against a thousand of Somerled's men (neither figure probably being intended to be very precise, and both for once perhaps being underestimates), the former nevertheless made an attack on the invaders. The *Carmen* then goes on to describe burning bushes and clouds of smoke, after which 'the baleful leader', in other words Somerled, fell at the first clash of arms, 'wounded by a spear thrown, slain by the sword'. Then, immediately after his death, his men took to flight and 'were slaughtered, both at sea and on land'. Many were drowned trying to board their ships, while the 'raging waves' swallowed up Somerled's son and many of the wounded. It seems from this account that the defenders attacked unexpectedly before Somerled's superior force could deploy for battle, under cover of a smokescreen produced either by burning wood and brush collected for the purpose or perhaps, if the weather was dry, by setting fire to the heather. Ironically Somerled's opponents were employing a tactic which he himself had used in his campaign in Morvern, if the MacDonald tradition is to be believed; taking advantage of the idea that men who were surprised near to their ships would fight less determinedly because they knew that a means of retreat was available. The defenders' plan was well thought out and it would be interesting to know who was responsible for it, but William, in common with most mediaeval chroniclers, is less concerned with the victory as a triumph of human ingenuity than as evidence of the favour of God and St Mungo, the patron saint of Glasgow.

The death of Somerled

Somerled himself no doubt pushed his way forward as soon as the attack materialised, eager as usual to lead from the front, only to be struck by a spear, presumably thrown from a distance before the battle lines clashed. Someone then rushed forward and finished him off with a sword stroke before his bodyguards could get him away to safety, and the news of his death spread quickly among the already shaken Islemen. The result was a stampede for the ships in which many of them were killed and wounded by their pursuers, striking with impunity at their vulnerable backs. But when they got to the shore some of the wounded were too badly injured to board the galleys, while others fell into the water in their haste and were drowned. William of Glasgow's 'raging wave' seems a rather exaggerated description for this sheltered stretch of the Clyde, but a combination of wind and tide might have made boarding hazardous, and men wearing armour would have found it difficult to scramble to safety even without the threat from their pursuers. Among the 'thousands' who drowned, says William, was Somerled's son. This cannot have been one of his three legitimate sons by Ragnhild, who are all known to have survived him, but the *Annals of Tigernach* confirm that a son named Gillebrichte did die with him. Somerled's corpse was decapitated by a priest, who personally handed the head to the bishop of Glasgow.

The later MacDonald histories provide a quite different version of events, accusing Somerled's nephew Maurice MacNeill of treacherously stabbing him to death during a private interview before the battle, having been bribed to do so by the king's councillors. According to this version the invading army was not defeated in battle, but simply dispersed on learning of their leader's death. It is understandable that Somerled's descendants would have sought an explanation for his sudden and unexpected overthrow, but this one cannot be taken seriously. It is not attested before the late seventeenth century, while all the earlier accounts agree that the great warrior was in fact killed in combat. *Orkneyinga Saga* admittedly confuses things still further by relating a story of how a Scot named Gilla Odran fled from Caithness after a murder and took refuge with a chief whom the saga calls Sumarlidi 'the Yeoman'. This character is described as ruler of Argyll, and as being married to Ragnhild, the daughter of King Olaf 'of the Hebrides', so there can be no doubt that he is the historical Somerled, or has at least been confused with him by the saga writer. But then we are told that Earl Rognvald of Orkney sent the notorious Svein Asleifsson, whom we have already encountered in Chapter 4, to hunt down Gilla Odran, and in two fierce sea battles Svein killed not only the fugitive, but also Sumarlidi himself before returning to report to a 'delighted' Rognvald. As Earl Rognvald Kali Kolsson of Orkney was killed in August 1158, six years before the Battle of Renfrew, the chronology alone makes it necessary to dismiss this account, which is not supported by any other evidence. All we can say is that the saga probably misidentified another Somerled or Sumarlidi (the name being by no means rare in the Norse-Gaelic community), and that this is far from being the only occasion on which the feats of Svein Asleifsson have been exaggerated.

Surprisingly, after its initial mutilation the body of Somerled seems to have been treated with considerable respect by the victors. Hugh MacDonald cites 'twenty writers in Icollumkill' – the island of Iona where the kings of Scots and of Man were traditionally buried – as stating that King Malcolm sent a boat to take the corpse there. As all these writers were said to have lived before the sixteenth-century accounts of Buchanan and Boetius they obviously represent an early tradition, though we do not know where Hugh had obtained his information. Several other sites have been claimed as Somerled's last resting place, notably the abbey at Saddell in Kintyre which he had reputedly founded, but there seems no reason to doubt the MacDonald version. The *Annals of Ulster* suggest that Somerled had a close connection with the church on Iona during his lifetime, as under the year 1164 it mentions that the abbacy of Iona had been offered to the Abbot of Derry 'on the advice of Somerled and the men of Argyll'. It may also be significant that in later years Somerled's son Ranald established two monasteries on the island. The choice of site also implies that King Malcolm did not entirely share William of Glasgow's view that the dead man had been a mere traitor. It is perhaps relevant that in the pro-Scottish *Melrose Chronicle* he is given the title of 'regulus Eregeithel' or 'regulus of Argyll'. The term 'regulus' implies a sub-king, a leader of admittedly royal rank, but who is also subject to a higher king. On the assumption that the chronicle represents something like an 'official' Scottish view of events, it is perhaps reasonable to deduce that Malcolm accepted that Somerled was of equivalent status to royalty, and so deserving of interment on the sacred isle.

Somerled's legacy

The claim has often been made that Somerled represented the resurgence of the Gaelic as opposed to the Scandinavian influence in western Scotland, and that his career was instrumental in the replacement of the latter by the native Celtic culture that it had temporarily submerged. In fact, as Somerled's biographer John Marsden has emphasised, by the twelfth century the two elements had become so intermingled that the contrast would have seemed meaningless to the great war leader and his contemporaries. Somerled and the kings of Man both represented the people of mixed Norse and Gaelic culture who had become known as 'Gall Gaidhil' or 'foreign Gaels', and their feuds were more of a local power struggle than an epic clash of cultures. But Somerled's descendants did include the founders of several powerful clans which were later to figure prominently in Gaelic resistance to the centralising policies of the kings of Scots, and their illustrious ancestor was naturally co-opted as a symbol of their beleaguered language and threatened independence. The clan of his eldest son, Dugall, became the MacDougalls, whose power base was in Ardnamurchan, Mull and Lorn. In the early fourteenth century they made the mistake of supporting the Comyn family who opposed Robert the Bruce in the Wars of Independence, and when Robert retreated to the west after his defeat at the Battle of Methven in 1306 he was surprised by a MacDougall army at Dalrigh near Tyndrum and the remnants of his forces put to flight. Robert returned two years later and crushed the MacDougalls at the Pass of Brander, after which their lands were confiscated and divided between the Campbells and the followers of Angus Og MacDonald, a descendant of Somerled's second son Ranald. The MacDougalls did partially restore their fortunes in the mid-fourteenth century under King David II, but the clan's dominant position in the Isles was taken over by the MacDonalds, who had remained loyal to King Robert and had distinguished themselves at Bannockburn. By 1336 John MacDonald of Islay was styling himself 'Dominus Insularum' or 'Lord of the Isles', and ten years later he made that boast a reality by marrying Amy MacRuari, heiress to the lands of the MacRuaris, who were also descended from Somerled's son Ranald.

This marriage brought almost the whole of the Hebrides under John's control, and for the next century and a half the MacDonald Lords of the Isles ruled from their base at Finlaggan on Islay as effectively independent rulers, the Norwegian kings having been removed from the equation after the Battle of Largs in 1263 (see Chapter 8). The MacDonalds strengthened their claim to legitimacy among the Gaelic-speaking islanders by emphasising their descent from the great Somerled, while in political terms they routinely safeguarded their position by playing off the English and Scottish monarchies against each other. At various times they also held the title of Earl of Ross, by which they extended their power across the north of Scotland as far as the east coast, and it was a dispute over this earldom which led to their most spectacular incursion onto the mainland in 1411, when an army led by Donald MacDonald was only turned back after a desperate fight at Harlaw, a day's march from Aberdeen. MacDonald fleets even raided as far as Ireland, where Raphael Holinshed recorded a great sea battle in 1400 in which the English were defeated by the nephew of the MacDonald chief, 'Red Hector of the Battles' MacLean. Nevertheless the kings in Edinburgh (who since 1371 had been members of the Stewart family descended from Walter fitz Alan) still considered that the Lord of the Isles held his possessions as a vassal of the monarchy, and so owed allegiance to them. For a while this vague arrangement sufficed despite regular 'revolts' (as the Scots kings saw it) on the part of the MacDonalds, but in the 1470s John MacDonald II finally overreached himself. He had opened negotiations with Edward IV in England, and by the secret Treaty of Ardtornish the two parties proposed to partition Scotland between themselves. The Scottish King James III discovered this during the course of his own negotiations, and not surprisingly regarded it as treason. Over the next decade he unleashed his own supporters against Clan Donald in a series of bloody campaigns which culminated in the overthrow of the Lordship. John, the last Lord of the Isles, was deposed in 1493 and died in obscurity. Unfortunately for the Stewart kings, they lacked the resources to replace the MacDonalds with anyone else capable of maintaining order in the West Highlands and Islands, and the outcome was the 'Age of Raids' of the sixteenth century, in which rival clans settled old scores in a multi-sided bloodbath. Clan warfare was nothing new, but this was on a very different scale from the traditional cattle-stealing, and resulted in the dispossession and virtual extermination of many of the weaker clans over the next century. At the same time the Hebrides, once at the centre of the lucrative trade routes between Norway and Ireland, became more geographically marginalised and economically weakened. Then, by the beginning of the seventeenth century, the aggressive policy of James VI saw even such powerful clans as the MacDonalds and the MacLeods of Lewis dispossessed of their lands, or at least deprived of the great galley fleets which had once symbolised their power. Understandably the Gaelic culture of this period was marked by a pronounced nostalgia for the period of the Lords of the Isles, and it is against this background that the first written MacDonald histories presented their heroic view of the lordship's founder, Somerled: or, as he had come to be known, Somhairle Mor, 'Somerled the Great'.

The battle sites today

Assuming that the Epiphany Battle of 1156 did take place in the Sound of Islay as suggested, the site was probably near the narrowest point of the strait, close to where Port Askaig on Islay now stands. The village is served by ferries from Kintyre and Colonsay, as well as by the short crossing of the Sound to Feolin Ferry on Jura. All these routes offer excellent views of the area. About two miles inland from Port Askaig is Loch Finlaggan, now the site of an interesting visitor centre, where the MacDonald Lords of the Isles had their headquarters. On the island of Am Fraoch Eilean ('Heather Island'), just off the coast of Jura at the southern end of the Sound (to starboard coming from Kintyre, grid reference NR472627), are the ruins of Claig Castle. This was a fortress once garrisoned by the Lords of the Isles to control the entrance to the strait, but it is not known whether it existed in the twelfth century, and there is little to be seen there today. The traditional slogan or war cry of Clan Donald, '*Fraoch Eilean*', may be derived from this place, though the place name is quite common in the Hebrides.

   The whole area around Renfrew where the battle of 1164 was fought is now built up, and although the general area of the battlefield can be identified, there is little to be seen today. The most likely site is now buried underneath the massive Braehead shopping centre (grid reference NS521674), but it is possible to walk from there along the south bank of the River Clyde, where Somerled's ships must have moored. Braehead is just east of Renfrew town centre, and there is a regular bus service from there. The exact location of the original monument on The Knock has been lost, but there is a modern stone cairn (erected in the 1950s) known as 'The Marjorie Bruce Cairn' at the junction of Renfrew Road and Dundonald Road in Paisley (grid reference NS489653).

Chapter 6

The Forgotten Field of Mam Garvia

Date: 31 July 1187
Location: Strath Garve, Easter Ross
Combatants: Royalist Scottish troops under Roland, lord of Galloway versus Donald Ban MacWilliam
Outcome: Royalist victory

The Scottish monarchy and the succession

Unlike the conflicts we have discussed so far, which pitted Norse or Norse-influenced Gaelic armies against either the Scottish kings or each other, the Battle of Mam Garvia was part of a long-running dynastic struggle, with the throne of Scotland itself as its goal. In order to understand why this conflict was so protracted and bloody it is necessary to look briefly at the much-debated question of the nature of the Scottish monarchy. Although the whole question is controversial, we can broadly accept Professor Barrow's view that there were two different traditions of kingship in early mediaeval Europe. One, typified (if not actually invented) by the Normans, saw the king as the head of the feudal pyramid, his authority based primarily on the control of land and inherited, like property in general, by the system of primogeniture, in other words from father to eldest son. This was the approach taken by the Norman and Angevin kings of England after 1066, and although ultimately based on ideas derived from Roman law, their model was concerned basically with power politics. As Barrow puts it, 'The king was king because he ruled, and ruled because he was king.' (Barrow, 1992). The Scots, however, like the contemporary Capetian rulers of France, adhered to an older tradition of sacred kingship, in which although the monarch was required to be of royal blood, he was at least in theory selected by his leading subjects from among a group of eligible candidates. It was therefore his own personal qualities – and crucially the agreement and acclamation of his people – that made him fit to rule. The bishop of Ross explained the difference eloquently in his *History of Scotland*, published in 1596: 'the kings were not called of Scotland as of the bare earth or a thing spiritless, but king of men, as King of Scots, as if the greater hope of their health they had in the men themselves, than in their land or silver'. Contrary to the claims sometimes made for the Scottish system, there was nothing particularly Celtic about it, and it was in fact very similar to that of the early Anglo–Saxon kings in England. An aspect which was particularly associated with the Scots and Irish, however, was what was known as the system of tanistry, whereby a deputy ruler or heir apparent was selected from among the eligible kin group (or *'derbfhine'*) during the current ruler's lifetime. In theory the 'tanaiste', as the appointee was called, would be the best qualified to succeed, but the system was often used as a way of balancing the claims of rival branches of the *derbfhine* by selecting their nominees alternately.

Of course none of these distinctions were ever absolute in practice, and no real monarchy ever fitted exactly with any idealised theory, but it is clear from the events of the twelfth century that there was room for legitimate disagreement in Scotland about the best candidate for the kingship in a way that would have been totally foreign to the Anglo–Normans. Unfortunately, a drawback of the tanaiste system is that over time the possible candidates tend to multiply, giving rise to an increasing risk of conflict among them and their respective branches of the family. No doubt less respectable motives also came into play. An eighteenth–century observer remarked of Somerled's descendants, the MacDonalds, that although they claimed to support the Stewart dynasty 'from a principle of honour and duty', in fact throughout their history they and other clans 'have been mostly loyal to some king or other who was not in possession, but seldom to any king on the throne' (A. Lang, quoted in Worton, 2018). The reason was a dislike of centralised royal authority in general, which they feared would curtail their traditional raiding, and there is no reason to suppose that things were any different in that respect in the twelfth century.

The MacHeths and the MacWilliams

The roots of the twelfth-century disputes over the throne went back to the events of 1057–1058, when Malcolm III 'Canmore' had taken the throne by defeating and killing first MacBeth and then the latter's stepson and successor, Lulach. Malcolm probably intended his eldest son Edward to succeed him, but both were killed in a surprise attack by Anglo-Norman cavalry at Alnwick in 1093 and the throne passed, after the brief reign of Donald III, to four of Malcolm's younger sons in succession: Duncan II, Edgar, Alexander I and David I, who succeeded in 1124. However, MacBeth's line had not been wiped out, because Lulach had left a son, Maelsnechtai, who seems at least for a time to have been accepted by Malcolm as Mormaer of Moray. Royal expeditions went north in 1078 and again in 1116 to reassert the authority of the monarchy, but Moray was still in the hands of Lulach's descendants in 1130, when the absence of King David in England encouraged them to revolt. The leaders of the rebellion were the mormaer Oengus, whom the *Annals of Ulster* describe as a grandson of Lulach, and a certain Malcolm. The latter is usually presumed to be the same person as Malcolm Mac Alasdair, who according to Orderic Vitalis was an illegitimate son of King Alexander I, and had rebelled against David soon after his accession in 1124. The objective of the revolt of 1130 is not certain. It is quite possible that both Oengus and Malcolm believed themselves to have a legitimate claim to the Scottish throne, although if Malcolm was not the son of King Alexander we do not know what his claim might have been. However, the rebels were defeated at the Battle of Stracathro, near Brechin in Augus, by a Scottish army led by the Constable of Scotland, Edward Siwardsson. Orderic says that 4,000 out of 5,000 Moray men were killed. Oengus was among the dead, but Malcolm escaped, only to be hunted down four years later. A chance remark by Ailred of Rievaulx, reporting a boast made by Robert de Brus of Annandale at the Battle of the Standard in 1138, tells us that David had asked Walter Espec, the high sherriff of Yorkshire, and other Anglo–Norman barons for help, and that they had mustered ships and men at Carlisle and harried Malcolm's followers until they handed him over in chains. Malcolm was imprisoned in Roxburgh Castle, but this did not mean the collapse of his cause; it was presumably his children whom the *Holyrood Chronicle* describes as making common cause with Somerled in rebelling against the new king Malcolm IV in 1153 (see Chapter 5).

After Stracathro Moray was at least briefly brought under royal control, before being granted to the king's nephew William, a son of Duncan II. There continues to be debate among historians over whether this William had a prior claim to the earldom of Moray, as it was now called, perhaps through marriage to a daughter of Maelsnechtai. Certainly his descendants, the MacWilliams, pursued a claim not only to Moray, but also to the Scottish throne itself: Bower relates how William's son, Donald Ban, boasted that he was 'of royal descent, the son of William, the son of Duncan the Bastard, the son of the great King Malcolm [Canmore], the husband of Saint Margaret.' However, Duncan II, whose brief reign ended in his death at the Battle of Mondyne, Kincardineshire, in 1094, was in fact not the son of Margaret, but of Malcolm's first wife Ingebjorg, the widow of none other than Thorfinn the Mighty, the earl of Orkney. Duncan had often been dismissed as illegitimate by Malcolm's other sons, his rivals for the kingship, though the grounds for this accusation are not altogether clear. It seems to have first been made by William of Malmesbury, and several Scottish chroniclers later followed his lead. It is possible that Ingebjorg had died before Malcolm's accession to the throne, which might have been a plausible pretext for ignoring their marriage, or at least for dismissing their offspring's claims to royal status. In the eyes of Margaret's descendants this would conveniently invalidate the claims of William and Donald Ban, but as we have seen there would have been many people in Scotland for whom the personal qualities of the rivals, or simply the right of a parallel branch of the family to be considered as eligible, were more important considerations than the strict rules of inheritance. Donald Ban's statement of his ancestry quoted above suggests that even if his grandfather was admitted to have been illegitimate, this did not in his own eyes invalidate his claim to 'royal descent'.

Also controversial is the question of the provenance of the Malcolm MacHeth who appears as if from nowhere in 1157, when the *Holyrood Chronicle* refers to his reconciliation with the throne, now occupied by David I's successor Malcolm. Traditionally it has been supposed that this Malcolm MacHeth was the same man who had been imprisoned at Roxburgh more than two decades earlier, and who had now been released in exchange for promises of fealty – or possibly as one of the terms of a peace treaty agreed between the king and Somerled, for which see Chapter 5. Some scholars have recently questioned this identification, pointing out for example that he could hardly have been the son of both Alexander and Heth, and that none of the sources which describe his activities before his capture in 1134 use the latter patronymic. But Professor R.A. MacDonald (2003) argues that it is unnecessary to posit the existence of two Malcolms when their activities both before 1134 and after 1157 are consistent with the policies of a single person. The confusion over names could then be resolved by accepting that Orderic Vitalis, our only source for Malcolm's descent from King Alexander, had simply made a mistake. He was, after all, writing from a distance in Normandy and was not always very well informed about Scottish affairs. Malcolm might then have more plausibly have been a relative of his fellow rebel Oengus of Moray. No one has yet succeeded in convincingly identifying his presumed father, Heth or Aed, although a man of that name appears as mormaer of Ross in some charters of David I's reign. After his release Malcolm seems to have been granted lands in the north, perhaps in recognition of his descent from this Aed and hence the validity of his claim to noble if not royal status, as the *Holyrood Chronicle* later refers to him as earl of Ross. (This is the first appearance in the records of this earldom, so Malcolm seems to have been part of the process by which the old mormaers were replaced with feudal earls. It may have been little more than a nominal title, as for much of the later twelfth century Ross was only intermittently under royal control.) If in fact the Malcolm who fought at Stracathro, the prisoner of Roxburgh and Earl Malcolm of Ross were the same person, this suggests that for at least thirty years the Kings of Scots had to live with the threat of insurrection from his branch of the ancient royal derbfhine, and – as discussed below – the last of the MacHeths was not suppressed until early in the following century.

The MacWilliam wars and the campaign of Mam Garvia

In the later twelfth century it was the MacWilliams who took up the role of chief rivals to the Canmore lineage. Malcolm IV died in 1165 and was succeeded by his younger brother William, whose impetuous and warlike nature earned him the Gaelic nickname of 'Garbh', which means harsh or rough. After his death he became better known as William 'the Lion', apparently because of the standard which he adopted (still the Royal Banner of Scotland today) bearing a red lion on a yellow ground. In 1173 William intervened in England in the civil wars between King Henry II and his sons, with the result that in the following year he was captured at Alnwick (surely a place of ill omen for the Canmore dynasty). He was released after the signing of the Treaty of Falaise in 1175, but the terms – which included the payment of a ransom and the subjection of the Scottish Church to the English – were seen by many as another humiliation for Scotland at the hands of Henry II, similar to that endured by his brother in 1159. Revolts broke out in several places, notably in Galloway in the south-west, where fighting continued until 1186. Roger of Howden describes how Donald Ban MacWilliam took advantage of the unrest by launching invasions of Scotland in both 1179 and 1181, and under the latter year remarks that Donald had 'many a time made incursions into that kingdom', which suggests that there were other such occasions not otherwise recorded. Walter Bower, in his fifteenth-century *Scotichronicon*, says that in the 1179 campaign the king responded to the threat by fortifying two bases in Ross, at Ederdour and Dunskeath. Dunskeath – not to be confused with Dunscaith Castle on the Isle of Skye – commands the north shore of the narrow entrance to the Cromarty Firth while Ederdour, now known as Redcastle, is on the southern shore of the Black Isle, overlooking the Beauly Firth. Between them they are well sited to protect the sea approaches to Ross and Moray from the north.

Presumably this strategy was successful for a time, because Donald Ban disappears again from the sources until 1186, when Bower describes how he returned and seized control of the earldom of Ross with the help of 'some disloyal subjects', whose identity is unfortunately not specified. Professor McDonald (2016) notes that a parchment roll once existed containing documents from the time of King William and his successor Alexander II, which listed both the magnates who sided with the kings and those 'who stood with MacWilliam'. This would have been a valuable source for this campaign, but unfortunately in 1296 it was taken, along with many other important documents, to England, where it was lost. The only named royal official known to have defected was the royal marshal Gillecolm, whom Bower says was captured when Donald Ban took the castle at Auldearn, near Nairn in Moray (Ross, 2007). According to Bower the rebels also occupied the whole of Moray, and subjected other parts of the kingdom to destructive raids. Roger of Howden gives the most detailed account of the subsequent campaign. A Scottish army led by several of the kingdom's leading earls marched north to Inverness, where it set up its headquarters. It is not clear whether the king himself was present, but if so he got no further than Inverness, uncharacteristically preferring to delegate the actual fighting to his subordinates. However, not all of them were eager to confront the MacWilliams, a fact which Howden attributes to disloyalty to the king, if not outright pro–MacWilliam sympathies: 'for certain of them loved the king not at all', he says. So the royalists sent out detachments to plunder those areas which were believed to support the rebels, while the main army remained in camp. But eventually – the date was Friday 31 July 1187 according to Bower's reckoning – one of these detachments ran into Donald Ban's army, quite possibly by accident. The exact location of the ensuing battle is not known precisely. The *Holyrood Chronicle* says that it was in Ross, while the *Melrose Chronicle* names a place which it calls 'Mam Garvia prope Muref', or 'Mam Garvia near Moray'. Professor Barrow (1992) has argued that a place which is 'in Ross' but 'near Moray' must presumably be somewhere to the north-west of Inverness, which marked the approximate boundary between the two earldoms at that time. The name Mam Garvia is Gaelic: 'Mam' in that language denotes a rounded hill, while 'Garbh' means rough (ironically, the same word that was applied to King William). An obvious candidate for the site, then, is the vicinity of the village of Garve in the valley or strath of that name, which runs from the high ground around Ben Wyvis towards the Cromarty Firth. It is about twenty miles from Inverness as the crow flies, so easily within reach of a mobile raiding party, and as the name implies it is in a mountainous area where a lightly equipped army might hope to find refuge. However, there are very many rounded hills in that vicinity, and much of the ground is indeed boggy, rocky or otherwise 'rough', so narrowing it down any further is likely to be impossible without some fortuitous archaeological discovery.

Two sources – the chronicle of Roger of Howden and Walter Bower's *Scotichronicon* – describe the battle in some detail, but their accounts differ in several important respects. In Bower's version the encounter happened by sheer luck:

> it chanced one day that when (the king) had sent out his men as usual, up to two thousand strong, to reconnoitre and take booty across the moors and countryside, some of those who were serving with the king's army suddenly and unexpectedly came upon MacWilliam as he was resting with his troops on a moor near Moray called 'Makgarby'.

Roger, however, implies that this was not just a random patrol; it consisted of 3,000 'warlike young men', led by Roland, the lord of Galloway, who had been sent out specifically to track down the rebels. In the twelfth century Galloway seems to have enjoyed a status similar to that of Somerled's Lordship of the Isles, largely autonomous but acknowledging – at least in theory – the overlordship of the king of Scots. Situated in the far south-west of Scotland, it had many features in common with the Hebrides, not least the culture of its people. The name Galloway, in fact, derives from 'Gall-Gaidhil', the same term that was applied to the mixed Norse-Celtic inhabitants of the Isles. Its soldiers had a reputation for ferocity in battle, but also for cruelty towards non-combatants; in the invasion of England that culminated in the Battle of the Standard in 1138, both Ailred of Rievaulx and Henry of Huntingdon accuse them of plundering churches, murdering women and children, and abducting people into slavery. In the mid-twelfth century Galloway was ruled by Fergus, styled 'ri' or king of Galloway, who is first attested as a witness of a charter issued by David I in 1136. From a genealogy given by Roger of Howden Fergus appears to have been married to an illegitimate daughter of Henry I of England, and had also married his own daughter to King Olaf of Man; he took advantage of these connections to play off the three neighbouring kingdoms against each other, and so is credited with avoiding total subjugation by the Scots, even though he supplied contingents for Scottish armies in campaigns like that of 1138. He stayed aloof during Somerled's wars against Scotland and Man, but was nevertheless deposed after an invasion by Malcolm IV in 1160, and died in exile at Holyrood Abbey in the following year. He was succeeded by his sons Uhtred and Gillebrigte, who at first acquiesced in the installation of Scottish garrisons and officials, but after King William's capture by the English in 1174 they rose in rebellion and drove them out. The brothers then fell out, and Gillebrigte captured Uhtred and had him blinded and castrated, as a result of which he died. Gillebrigte maintained his independence until his death in 1185, but then Uhtred's son Roland returned from exile, slaughtered those nobles who had supported his uncle, and established himself in the lordship. Following an armed standoff with King William he submitted to the latter's authority, after which he became a loyal vassal for the rest of his life.

The 'young men' of Galloway, therefore, were not only more trustworthy than the contingents of many of the other Scottish nobles, but were also battle-hardened warriors led by a man with previous military experience. Certainly they showed more aggressive spirit than most of their comrades in arms. 'And when they approached the army of the aforesaid MacWilliam' says Roger of Howden, 'they made an attack upon them, and slew MacWilliam [i.e. Donald Ban] himself and many of his army.' Again Bower's account is slightly different, because he says that it was the rebels who took the initiative and attacked:

> When MacWilliam saw that the king's troops were few in comparison with his own, he hurriedly joined battle with them, and charged the royal forces. They bravely resisted all his efforts, and because they trusted in the righteousness of their cause, continued to resist courageously. With God's help they cut down MacWilliam and five hundred of his men, and put the rest to flight, on Friday 31 July, thus repaying him with a just reward for his evil deeds.

Both chroniclers agree that the surviving rebels fled without delay after the death of Donald. The rebel leader's head was then cut off and taken to the king, who displayed it to the whole army as proof of the victory.

It is not easy to account for this surprise victory by a detachment of the royal army over an enemy who had previously been so hard to subdue. It is unlikely to have been due to any superiority in equipment on the part of Roland's men. It seems fair to assume that as 'lord of Galloway' he was leading a contingent raised in that territory, and even if they were accompanied by a hard core of armoured knights supplied by the king, the 'rough' terrain of Mam Garvia cannot have been very suitable for their mounted tactics. In his invasion of the country in 1185 Roger of Howden says that Roland led 'a numerous host of horse and foot', but the horse were probably a small percentage of the army. Ralph de Diceto, writing of another campaign in 1177, says that the men of Galloway went into battle on foot, some of them carrying long 'lances' which served both as weapons and as standards, the rest with throwing spears in their right hands and long knives in their left. This dual armament made it impossible for them to use a shield, and their customary lack of any defensive armour increased their vulnerability still further. The defeat of the Galwegians in the Scottish army at the Battle of the Standard in 1138 had been attributed to this lack of protection, because of which they suffered severe losses at the hands of English archers and dismounted knights. Neither were they especially well disciplined or tactically sophisticated. According to Henry of Huntingdon's account of the same battle they attacked not in disciplined formations but in 'scattered groups', while Ailred of Rievaulx describes them charging with 'a horrible yell' and slashing with their swords in 'blind madness'. No doubt they were accustomed to breaking the enemy at the first onslaught, aided by the psychological effect of this almost berserk fury. Their tactics would have been much more effective in a sudden surprise attack on an unsuspecting enemy, but Bower's account of Mam Garvia suggests that it was MacWilliam who, seeing that his men outnumbered the Galwegians, decided to join battle with them. Conversely, MacWilliam's 500 dead, though a serious loss, was not a disastrously high proportion of a force that was clearly much bigger than Roland's two or three thousand, so most of the rebels must have made their escape. This suggests that they turned to flight fairly quickly, perhaps in response to the fortuitous death of their leader in the first onset, just as had happened to Somerled's army at Renfrew.

The situation might be easier to visualise if we knew more about the composition of the rebel army. The *Barnwell Chronicle* says of Guthred MacWilliam's 1211 campaign that he was 'supported by Scots and Irish', and Fordun actually claims that that invasion was launched from Ireland, but these are the first mentions of Irish troops in this connection and, although they may have been present on earlier occasions, this must remain speculation. Bower mentions 'disloyal subjects' who helped MacWilliam to seize Ross in 1186, and

in 1211 more specifically accuses 'the thanes of Ross' of supporting
the rebels. The term 'thane' at this date usually denoted the manager
of a royal estate, so the accusation of disloyalty would be justified in
the case of these officials, but although we can be sure that some of
MacWilliam's army consisted of local men, on both the occasions
mentioned they seem to be relegated to a supporting role rather than
being the originators of the revolt. As for the men of Moray, who had
certainly been involved in the Stracathro campaign of 1130, there is
no evidence to link them with the later revolts of the MacWilliams.
Both Fordun and the *Melrose Chronicle* describe the Moravians, as
the inhabitants of Moray were known, as inveterate rebels, but no
contemporary source specifically says that they came out against
the king in either 1186 or 1211. In fact Bower refers several times
to rebel attacks on Moray, implying perhaps that the province was
targeted because of its loyalty to the king. Alasdair Ross (2007)
points out that the siting of the two royal castles at Ederdour and
Dunskeath strongly suggests that they were intended to protect Ross
against fleets coming from the north or east. This would have been a
very unlikely direction of approach for anyone coming from Ireland
or the Hebrides, since it would have been far easier to land on the
west coast and march overland than to risk the dangerous passage
around the north of Scotland and through the Pentland Firth. The
most likely source for an invader threatening Easter Ross from the
sea would therefore have been Orkney. Bearing in mind that Donald
Ban's grandfather Duncan II seems to have traced his descent from
Earl Thorfinn's widow Ingebjorg, Ross argues that the MacWilliams
could have had extensive family connections in Orkney, and that
Earl Harald Maddasson might even have deliberately harboured
them as useful allies in his own disputes with the Scots. In that case
it is quite possible that many of MacWilliam's best equipped and
most experienced soldiers were Orkney men, who probably closely
resembled the Lewis chessmen described in Chapter 1 and the mail-

armoured men described by Gerald de Barri at Dublin in 1171. If so their defeat at the hands of a smaller force of more lightly equipped Galwegians is even harder to explain. But battles, as mediaeval commanders well knew, were risky undertakings in which the role of sheer chance was always significant. And in dynastic wars such as this, in which the death of a single man could decide the issue on the spot, the vulnerability of a chief whose culture required him to lead from the front could have calamitous consequences.

The revolt of 1210 and the end of the MacWilliams

Mam Garvia, however, was not the end of the wars between the MacWilliams and the kings of Scots. Donald Ban was dead, but his son Guthred kept the cause alive, and if the MacWilliams had not already possessed bases in the Hebrides and Ireland at the time of the Mam Garvia campaign, they appear to have acquired them by 1210, and they must have compensated to a large extent for the loss of the Orkney base of operations after the death of Harald Maddadsson in 1206. In 1210 Guthred invaded Ross, invited, according to Bower, by treacherous local thanes as part of another plot to overthrow the king. William the Lion was still on the throne, but he must by then have been nearly seventy years old and his grip on power was slackening. In the following year he led a large army into Ross, where he is said to have rebuilt the two castles at Ederdour and Dunskeath which had originally been fortified in the 1179 campaign. From these bases the king sent out expeditionary forces, just as he had done in 1187, which harried Guthred's supporters wherever he could find them. But Guthred resorted to guerrilla warfare, avoiding contact with the royal army while he ambushed patrols and ran off cattle as the opportunity offered. The king therefore sent out a mobile force of 4,000 men, led by the earls of Atholl and Buchan, to hunt down the enemy in his mountain hideout.

This tactic sounds as if it could have been a deliberate attempt to repeat the success of the Galwegians at Mam Garvia, but on this occasion it was less than decisive. The earls discovered Guthred's headquarters on an island, whose whereabouts Bower does not specify, but which may have been on one of the many freshwater lochs in Ross. In the ensuing battle the stronghold was taken and many of the rebels were killed, but Guthred was not among them. The rebel leader had managed to escape and take refuge with his surviving men in a nearby forest. At Michaelmas the king, perhaps believing that the rebels had been decisively defeated, returned south with the main army and left Malcolm, the earl of Fife, to hold Moray. However, as soon as the royal army had left, Guthred emerged from hiding and besieged one of the castles that William had built in Ross. According to Walter Bower he 'made ready his siege engines' and threatened to launch an attack, but the garrison offered to surrender in exchange for their lives. Guthred granted this, but burned the castle to the ground. A couple of interesting points emerge here regarding the warfare of the period. The castle, like those erected by the Normans in England immediately after the conquest of 1066, was presumably made of timber, which was much cheaper and quicker to build with than stone. The oldest mediaeval stone castle in Scotland is probably the ruin known as 'Cubbie Roo's Castle' in Orkney, built by Kolbein Hruga in the 1140s, but stone construction was by no means yet universal. Nevertheless, the fact that Guthred possessed siege engines able to threaten even a wooden fortification suggests that the armies of the MacWilliams were not the hordes of unsophisticated barbarians that their enemies often implied. We do not know what sort of engines they were, but battering rams and rope-powered stone-throwers made of wood like those in widespread use elsewhere in Europe would have been fairly easy to construct, and light enough to be transported over the difficult country in which the rebels operated.

Earl Malcolm either went voluntarily to report to the king or was summoned to court, which cannot have been a pleasant experience as William was reported to be furious at the loss of the castle. Winter was now approaching, and it was impossible to rectify the situation at once. But the next summer an army under the king's son Alexander was sent north from Lothian to Ross, William himself intending to follow close behind with the main royal army. However, in the meantime Guthred was betrayed by his own followers, perhaps weary of the constant guerrilla warfare, and handed over to the earl of Buchan, the king's justiciar, who had been left in charge in Moray during Malcolm's absence. The earl put Guthred in chains and took him to Kincardine with the idea of handing him over to William, but the prisoner was on hunger strike and was by then very weak. When he learned that the king did not want to meet his rival, his captor therefore beheaded him and hung up his body so that all could see that the pretender to the throne was dead. The king then sent the earl of Atholl to Ireland where he ravaged Donegal, a response which suggests that the people of this region were known to have supported the MacWilliams, or at least were the source of some of their recruits.

This was still not quite the last of the MacWilliams, however, for on the death of William the Lion in 1214 they once again revolted against his son Alexander II. On this occasion their leaders were Guthred's brother, another Donald Ban, and a certain Kenneth MacHeth, who had emerged from obscurity as the last representative of another lineage of would-be kings. Kenneth's genealogy is unknown, but he was probably the son or grandson of the Malcolm MacHeth who had been Earl of Ross in the previous century. But the power of both factions was in decline, and even the last-minute alliance between them did not provide the military power necessary to threaten the monarchy. Local loyalists in Ross were able to deal with the insurrection without the aid of the royal army. Their leader was Farquhar MacTaggart (Fearchair mac an t'sagairt, or 'son of the priest'), who was to become an important ally of the monarchy in the north. He defeated and killed both Donald and Kenneth and sent their heads to the king, who granted him a knighthood. Twenty years later Farquhar was to be appointed earl of Ross, the position once held by his enemies.

The very last act in the long-running saga came in 1228, when yet another desperate incursion by the MacWilliams, probably launched from the Hebrides, led to the capture of Abertarff Castle, near present-day Fort Augustus at the southern end of Loch Ness. Their commanders were now Gilleasbuig MacWilliam and a certain Ruaraidh, plausibly identified by J.L. Roberts (1997) with the son of Ranald, king of the Isles, who was himself a son of Somerled. Perhaps if the MacWilliams and the lords of the Isles had made common cause against the Scots in the previous century they might have enjoyed more success, but by now it was too late. Just as in 1214, the kingdom was now strong enough to leave the suppression of these revolts to local forces. Although they succeeded in burning Inverness and doing a great deal of damage to the surrounding countryside, Gilleasbuig and Ruaraidh were quickly defeated by the earl of Buchan, William Comyn. Walter Bower reports that Gilleasbuig and his two sons were killed in the following year, which left Gilleasbuig's infant daughter as the only surviving member of the MacWilliam dynasty. The English *Lanercost Chronicle* tells how in 1230, on the orders of King Alexander II, she was taken to Forfar, where a proclamation was read out in an attempt to give the appearance of legal process. Then the little girl was picked up and her brains were dashed out against the market cross. Even the Lanercost chronicler, generally favourable to the Scottish kings, described this horrific act as 'too cruel', but it did finally bring to an end 100 years of dynastic strife.

Locating Mam Garvia

Of all the battlefields discussed in this book, Mam Garvia is the most elusive. No contemporary source gives a precise location; there are hints from which the general area can be deduced, but the actual battlefield may never be identified unless some future archaeological discoveries enable us to pinpoint it more precisely. But such a stroke of luck is unlikely, given that – as Tony Pollard (2012) points out – no artefacts that can be definitely associated with the battle have been recovered even from such a well-studied site as Bannockburn. The village of Garve (grid reference NH394615) is on the Black Water River about 12 miles west of Dingwall, on the A835 from Dingwall to Ullapool. It is also served by a station on the Inverness to Kyle of Lochalsh railway, regarded as one of the great scenic rail journeys of Scotland. Just west of Garve the railway and the A832 leave the Ullapool road and turn west along Strath Bran towards Loch Carron on the west coast. This is the most likely route by which troops from the Hebrides and Ireland would have marched to Easter Ross.

The ruins of several of the castles which featured in the MacWilliam Wars survive and can be visited. Dunskeath (grid reference NH807690) is about a mile east of Nigg Ferry on the north shore of the Cromarty Firth. It can be reached by road, but a quicker and more direct route is by the ferry from Cromarty on the Black Isle, which runs from June to September. The present building at Redcastle stands on the site of William the Lion's Ederdour Castle, but dates from the seventeenth century. It is now in a ruinous state and unsafe to enter. It is situated just east of the village of Milton, off the A832 from Muir of Ord to Cromarty (grid reference NH584495). At the western end of the village of Auldearn (grid reference NH917556), two miles east of Nairn on the A96 from Inverness, are the remains of the motte of the castle built by William the Lion and captured by Donald Ban MacWilliam during the Mam Garvia campaign. Follow the signs to the Boath Doocot, a seventeenth-century dovecote on the site.

Chapter 7

Clairdon – the Last Viking Battle

Date: 1198
Location: Clairdon, near Thurso, Caithness
Combatants: Orkney men under Earl Harald Maddadsson versus
  men of Caithness led by Harald 'the Young'
Outcome: Orkney victory

Harald 'the Old'

In 1190 the earldom of Orkney was still firmly in the hands of Harald Maddadsson, the son of Earl Maddad of Atholl and his wife Margaret, whose plot against Earl Paul was described in Chapter 4. Harald's claim to Orkney was derived from his mother, who was the daughter of Earl Haakon Paulsson who had ruled from 1104 until 1123. There is little doubt that the Scottish king David I had helped to engineer Harald's appointment as joint earl in 1139, when Harald was only five years old, with the aim of weakening the earldom and paving the way for a Scottish takeover of its mainland possessions in Caithness, if not of Orkney itself. But for nearly sixty years Harald had maintained his independence, cleverly playing off the kings of Scotland and Norway, as well as numerous pretenders to both thrones, against each other, and had earned by his endurance the nickname of 'Harald the Old'. There seems little doubt, in fact, that he had not confined himself to defending his own earldom, but had repeatedly meddled in the internal affairs of both Scotland and Norway. It may have seemed to him that only by weakening his powerful neighbours could he hope to maintain his freedom of action, but although he appeared to be successful in the short term, the hostility of the royal house of Scotland would ultimately bring his dynasty to an end. Nine years after he attained the position of sole earl in 1158 Harald divorced his first wife, the daughter of the Scottish earl of Fife, and married Hvarflod, a daughter of Malcolm MacHeth (whose career is discussed in Chapter 6). Whether his new wife was the cause or merely a symptom of a change of policy is not certain, but the *Gesta Annalia* implies the former. It tells us that until the marriage Harald had been a reliable vassal of the Scottish kings, but that this changed immediately afterwards. At about the same time Malcolm MacHeth died, and it is possible that Harald now saw himself as his father-in-law's natural successor as earl of Ross.

There seems to be no hard evidence that Harald interfered directly in the rebellion of the MacWilliams (though see the discussion in Chapter 6 above), but even if his own troops were not involved in the battle, the defeat of Donald Ban MacWilliam at Mam Garvia in 1187 left him dangerously exposed to a now-hostile Scottish kingdom. It is not clear, however, that the earl himself realised the full implications of the shift in the balance of power further south. He continued to act as if his earldom was an independent power on the international stage, even embarking on a risky foray into Norwegian politics. In 1193 Harald backed a rebellion against King Sverrir of Norway by the supporters of Sigurd, a son of the previous ruler Magnus Erlingsson, who had been overthrown and killed nine years earlier. The rebels were known as the '*Eyiarskeggjar*' or 'Island beardies', apparently in recognition of the fact that many of them came from Orkney and the Hebrides, where the modern fashion of shaving the beard had not yet been adopted as it had in Norway. The 'beardies' were crushed at the Battle of Floruvoe, near Bergen, and Harald was forced to travel to Norway and throw himself on the king's mercy. *Sverrir's Saga* tells how the earl tried to excuse himself by claiming that because of his advanced age he was no longer able to control Orkney as he once had, and that his rebellious subjects, who had got into the habit of plundering at will in Scotland and Ireland, had sailed for Norway without his permission. The king eventually agreed to pardon him, but confiscated the lands of the rebels and appointed royal officials to administer them. He also took the Shetland Islands under his own control, and decreed that half of the fines levied from those who broke the law in Orkney should now go directly to Norway. This of course not only reduced Harald's revenue, but also installed in Orkney a group of men loyal to Sverrir who could keep an eye on the earl's activities. Harald naturally resented this, and after Sverrir's death in 1202 he had the officials assassinated and regained much of his freedom of action in Orkney. The loss of Shetland, however, was effectively permanent, although Norwegian sources suggest that Harald might have regained control there for a brief period after Sverrir's death. After that the islands remained subject to the Norwegian monarchy until 1468, when Christian I, now king of Denmark and Norway, pawned them to James II of Scotland in lieu of a dowry for his daughter.

On his return from Norway, far from learning his lesson, Earl Harald compounded his problems by interfering once again in Scottish affairs. He probably considered that the greatest threat to his position came from the de Moravia family in Moray, the descendants of Freskin, the Flemish nobleman who had been installed there by David I in the 1130s. Since then the family had also been awarded lands in Ross, thus encroaching even closer to Caithness. Harald may also have felt threatened by the castles which William the Lion had established at Ederdour and Dunskeath during his 1179 expedition, which were well positioned, whether by design or not, to deny him access to the timber resources of Easter Ross. Whatever the reason, an army from Orkney invaded Moray in 1196, when Harald's son Thorfinn fought a battle at Inverness. In the following year a Scottish royal army retaliated by advancing into Caithness, but Roger of Howden says that Harald was reluctant to confront the king's forces directly, and so they were able to advance unopposed as far as Thurso, where they destroyed the earl's castle before returning south. *Orkneyinga Saga* understandably glosses over the subsequent events, but Roger of Howden and the *Melrose Chronicle* help to fill in the gaps. It appears that Harald agreed to negotiate and provide hostages, including his son Thorfinn, but when the hostages failed to materialise William took the earl himself prisoner to Edinburgh until Thorfinn was handed over. In effect Harald was acknowledging, as several of his predecessors had, that he held Caithness – though not Orkney – as a subordinate of the king of Scots. The difference on this occasion was that the king was able to enforce the agreement by military force. It was in fact the first recorded occasion (discounting the affair at Duncansby discussed in Chapter 2) on which a Scottish royal army reached the north coast. This should have sent a clear warning to Harald that he could no longer rely on having a secure base on the mainland.

King William was still not strong enough to risk war with Norway by taking the fight to Harald in Orkney, but another opportunity had now presented itself in the form of a rival claimant to the earldom. This was another Harald, nicknamed 'Ungi' or 'the Young', whose claim was based on the fact that he was a grandson of Harald the Old's former co-ruler, Earl Rognvald. *Orkneyinga Saga* describes how some years before this Harald Ungi had travelled to Norway, where the then king, Magnus Erlingsson, had recognised him as the rightful earl, and had then gone via Shetland and Caithness to Scotland, where King William granted him the half of Caithness which had once belonged to Rognvald. The legal basis on which William made such a grant is uncertain, since he had apparently accepted the homage of Harald Maddadsson for the whole of Caithness, but the king was no doubt happy to seize any opportunity to neutralise his old enemy.

Harald Ungi then returned to his new fief, which he clearly intended to use as a base from which to take over the whole of the earldom. He was joined there by his brother-in-law Lifolf, known as 'Bald Pate', who made use of his extensive local connections to raise troops on his behalf. Lifolf was then despatched to Orkney to demand that Harald Maddasson should not only recognise his rival's claim to lands in Caithness, but also hand over half of the islands. Another recruit to young Harald's cause was Sigurd Mite, a young man whom the saga describes as handsome and extravagant, but who must also have commanded a significant local following. Harald Ungi's father had been brought up in Sutherland, and may have held land there from which further troops could be levied. It seems fairly certain, then, that the pretender enjoyed considerable support on the mainland, but the men of Orkney remained loyal to their existing earl. Relying on their support Harald Maddadsson refused to negotiate, but instead raised his own army and led it in person to the mainland to confront his enemy.

The Battle of Clairdon

The issue was settled in 1198 somewhere on the coast of Caithness, in what was probably the last full-scale Viking-style battle fought on British soil. The site of the battle has never been definitively established. There is an edifice on a hill north-east of Thurso which has traditionally been known as Harold's Tower; it was in fact built in around 1780 by local landowner Sir John Sinclair as a family burial vault, but several local historians record traditions linking it to the battle and to the site of the death of Harald the Young. According to Donald Grant in *Old Thurso*, it was built on the site of a much older chapel, which marked the 'commonly accepted place of Harald's death'. Falconer Waters refers to the tower as being built on the spot where Harald 'was said to have been killed at the Battle of Clairdon'.

Clairdon or Clardon is a small farming settlement about a mile to the east of the tower, whose name is often used for the battle, on the assumption that this location is at least approximately the correct one. James Gray, writing in 1922, confirms that the battle was 'said to have been fought at Clairdon'. Unfortunately the site has never been excavated, and the existence of a local tradition in the twentieth century is of little use as evidence, because it cannot be proven to be independent of the main source, *Orkneyinga Saga*, which has been available in English since 1873. Barbara Crawford rejects it altogether, preferring the statements of the earlier king's saga *Fagrskinna* and the English chronicler Roger of Howden that the encounter was fought 'near Wick'.

Wick and Thurso – then as now the only sizeable towns in Caithness – are only about twenty-five miles apart, and from the perspective of a writer based in Iceland or Norway, 'near Thurso' and 'near Wick' need not be seen as mutually exclusive. *Orkneyinga Saga* itself is vague about the battle's location, but it does give us some clues which can help to narrow it down. Harald the Younger was with his army in Caithness when he sent Lifolf 'across the Pentland Firth' on a reconnaissance mission. Lifolf landed on South Ronaldsay and returned with discouraging news of the size of Earl Harald's forces, whereupon a discussion took place about the advisability of going to Thurso for reinforcements. This did not happen for unspecified reasons, but soon afterwards the enemy fleet was seen 'sailing close to the islands', prompting Harald the Young and the Caithness men to deploy for battle. The Orkney forces 'came ashore' and immediately joined battle. Young Harald was subsequently killed 'near some peat diggings' and a church was later built on the spot. He was buried 'on the headland', at a location which was presumably not far from where he died. So if we accept the reliability of this account (which is essentially the only one we have), our battle site has to meet the following criteria. It must be near to the Caithness coast, at a spot from which islands (presumably the Orkneys) are visible. It must be near enough to Thurso for the town to be an obvious source of troops, but not so accessible that the recruiting party could have been despatched there in the time available. It should be on or near a headland, in an area where peat was dug, and should be the site of a church or chapel.

In the vicinity of Wick there is an excellent beach at Sinclair's Bay where an army could land, as we saw in Chapter 2. The island of South Ronaldsay might be seen from there in unusually good visibility, although the distance is over twenty miles. But to march to Thurso and back from there would take several days, and would seem to be an entirely unnecessary excursion if a source of men was to be found in or around Wick. Other considerations suggest that the 'traditional' site at Clairdon is indeed the correct one. Thurso is visible from the hill at a distance of little more than a mile, but it is situated on the far side of the Thurso River, which is very susceptible to rapid rises in water level following rain on the high ground to the south. There is no record of a bridge in the Middle Ages, and in fact the ford by which the river was once crossed is still visible today, marked by stepping stones. It might have seemed an easy matter to send a detachment into Thurso, but the expedition would have had to be abandoned if it failed to find a safe way across. If this hypothesis is correct, Earl Harald's landing-place must have been the sandy beach at Murkle Bay, about three miles east of the site of the tower, and as we shall see there is reason to believe that the battle flowed westwards during the course of the day. South Ronaldsay is not visible from Clairdon, because of the intervening height of Dunnet Head, but the neighbouring island of Hoy can easily be seen from the coast around Thurso Bay. Clairdon does not look like an obvious headland on the map, but on the ground it is a prominent feature. This is especially the case when seen from Thurso, from where it appears to form a counterpart to Holborn Head on the opposite side of the bay. Peat does not appear to be dug there now, but the brown colour of the streams flowing off the hill is a clear indication that peat is present. And of course we have the tradition, vague though it is, of a chapel which predates the existing monument.

Orkneyinga Saga describes an epic fight in the old Viking style, complete with the traditional saga motifs. However, we should not necessarily imagine that the combatants looked exactly like their predecessors of earlier centuries. In this connection Barbara Crawford (2013) discusses the 'seal of the community of Orkney', which survives in some fragmentary fifteenth-century examples, but was probably originally granted in the thirteenth. It shows two figures, presumably representing members of the local elite, dressed in tight-fitting jerkins and breeches with embroidered bands round the collar, cuffs, waist and knees, and knee-length boots which Crawford believes are intended to represent sealskin. In fact she suggests that the jerkin and breeches might also have been sealskin, in which case they could have been tough enough to give some protection in combat. Apart from this, the nearest visual evidence in time and space comes from the Lewis chessmen, from which we can deduce that although Viking-style weapons – swords, spears and axes – remained in use, defensive equipment would have more closely resembled the styles in use elsewhere in Europe, with kite shields and kettle helmets at least partly replacing the old round shields and conical headgear. Nevertheless, the battle seems to have been fought on foot, between men drawn up in close-order lines in a way which would not have been unfamiliar to Sigurd the Mighty.

Also in the old Viking style, Lifolf and Sigurd Mite exchanged taunts before the fighting began, with the latter responding to Lifolf's suggestion that they wait for reinforcements with the remark that 'It's very sad when the earl's own brother-in-law crosses the Pentland Firth just to discover that he's left his guts behind.' Lifolf replied to the effect that self-proclaimed 'supermen' like Sigurd often failed to live up to their boasts when things got tough, and that his rival would be as quick as anyone to desert Harald if his cause seemed to be lost. Sigurd had tucked the hem of his scarlet tunic into his belt at the front and left it hanging loose at the back, but when his men pointed this out he refused to correct it, saying that the enemy would not be seeing his back that day. Sigurd and Lifolf each commanded a wing of Harald the Young's army; we are told nothing of Harald's own activities until the battle was over, and he may have decided to leave things to his two more experienced subordinates. According to the saga the army of Earl Harald the Old was 'much larger', and many of its warriors were 'tough and well equipped'. The saga writer especially singles out for mention 'the bishop's kinsmen' – the relatives and retainers, that is, of Bjarni Kolbeinsson, the bishop of Orkney and a personal friend of the earl, who is said to have had many kinsfolk in the islands – though we are not told that the bishop was present in person. When the lines clashed the men of Caithness fought ferociously, and probably had – at least at first – the advantage of the higher ground as Earl Harald's men fought their way uphill from Murkle Bay. But numbers eventually told, and Harald the Young's army was gradually forced westwards towards Thurso Bay. Perhaps we should envisage the earl's men making slow progress at first, temporarily forced back by repeated charges, but gathering momentum as they reached the crest and attacked downhill. We are told that Lifolf cut his way through the enemy ranks on three separate occasions, but clearly none of these attacks was decisive and he was eventually pushed back to his starting point. Donald Grant (1965) records a tradition that the Caithness men were forced back as far as 'The Crook', a stretch of shore on the far side of the Thurso River, and that a chapel was later built there in memory of young Harald. The lower course of the Thurso in this area has been straightened and dredged since, and the sea level is known to be higher now than it was in the Middle Ages, so it is perhaps not impossible that some men managed to fall back across the river here.

Nevertheless, most of the fighting must have taken place on the hill where Harald's Tower now stands, and it was here that Harald is said to have met his death. Sigurd Mite did live up to his boasts and fought 'like a true champion', but was eventually killed. About the same time Lifolf, of whom the saga says that he fought hardest of all, also 'died a hero's death'. With their leaders dead, the Caithness men scattered to their homes; it may of course have been at this stage that they crossed the river into Thurso, perhaps followed by a few of the more enthusiastic among their pursuers. Harald the Young was killed 'near some peat diggings', which might imply that he was caught hiding in a ditch rather than fighting to the last, but this did not prevent the local people from regarding him as a martyr. *Orkneyinga Saga* tells how that night a 'great light' was seen on the spot where he died, and a church was subsequently built there. It is not certain that this was the church which stood on the spot where the tower is now, but if this identification is correct the battle must have reached its climax on the western slope of the hill, in full view of the townsfolk of Thurso.

Dalharrold – the battle that never was?

Clairdon did indeed turn out to be the end of an era. Never again would the succession to the earldom of Orkney be decided by a pitched battle between the rival claimants. Instead the issue would be subsumed into the wider struggle between Scotland and Norway for control of the Isles. Temporarily frustrated, William the Lion sent messengers to Rognvald Godredsson, the king of Man, asking him to intervene. *Orkneyinga Saga* describes Rognvald, who reigned in Man from 1188 until 1226, as 'the greatest fighting man in all the western lands', a veteran campaigner who had spent three whole years on board ships without ever sleeping under a roof. Nevertheless, he had already seen the writing on the wall, and although still nominally subject to Norway he had quietly made his submission to the kings of both Scotland and England. He obediently raised an army from Ireland, Kintyre and the Hebrides and occupied Caithness, while Harold retired to Orkney and avoided all contact with him. James Gray, after giving an account of these events which is based mainly on *Orkneyinga Saga*, goes on to describe how Rognvald and Harold met in battle at Dalharrold in upper Strath Naver, in Sutherland. An alternative version, says Gray, has William the Lion himself in command at this encounter instead of Rognvald. Harold was allegedly defeated there and forced to retreat northwards down Strath Naver to the sea, from where he sailed back to Orkney. Gray admits that neither the saga nor any other near contemporary sources say anything about this battle, whose location 'rests solely on tradition', but this has not prevented numerous modern writers from presenting it as fact. For example, the Strath Naver Trail map, published by the Highland Council in Inverness in 2003, describes a battle between 'the Norse Earls of Orkney and the Kings of Scotland' at a site near the eastern end of Loch Naver, in which 'the Norsemen were defeated'. It is, however, by no means certain that this encounter is historical, or if it did occur, that it can be associated with this campaign. Dalharrold is in a remote location in the interior of the country, and is best known in archaeological circles for a Bronze Age stone circle known as Clach an Righ, or 'the king's stone'. In fact the concentration of prehistoric mounds and hut circles in this area suggests that they might have been responsible for the tradition of the battle in the first place. There are numerous instances in Scotland of much earlier remains being identified with battles against the Norsemen – see for example Peter Marren's discussion (Marren, 1990) of the 'Bloody Pits' at Gamrie near Banff, and the fictional encounter supposedly commemorated by Sueno's Stone at Forres. It is true that Dalharrold lies near what may have been the main overland route from the west coast, via the 'horse field' at Rosal (see Chapter 2) to the fertile valley of Strath

Naver, but this would not necessarily have been a logical itinerary for anyone intending to invade Caithness. In fact the implication of the *Orkneyinga Saga*'s remark about Rognvald spending three years sleeping on board ship is that he habitually campaigned by sea, and it would have surely been more logical for him to do so in this case, especially as his army of Islemen must have been transported by ship to wherever on the mainland they made their initial landing.

Harald strikes back

Rognvald briefly subjugated the whole of Caithness, but he only stayed for one winter before returning to the Hebrides with the bulk of his forces, leaving behind three stewards, Mani Olafsson, Rafn the Lawman, and Hlifolf the Old, to administer the province on behalf of King William. As soon as Rognvald had gone Earl Harald sent an assassin from Orkney to kill one or more of the stewards. *Orkneyinga Saga* tells how the assassin fell into the hands of Rafn, who interrogated him and discovered what his mission was, but refused to kill him as the man was a kinsman. Instead he was allowed to go free, after which he managed to murder Hlifolf before escaping back to Orkney. Possibly Rafn had engineered this deliberately as a way of eliminating a rival and consolidating power in his own hands, but if so his duplicity was in vain. In 1201 Harald landed at Thurso with a large fleet, captured the castle without resistance and drove out the stewards, who took refuge in Scotland. More seriously, however, the earl also captured the bishop of Caithness, John, who had arrived from his palace at Scrabster, about a mile from Thurso, and offered to negotiate. According to *Orkneyinga Saga* Harald had him blinded and his tongue cut out, then massacred all his guards. John's injuries might have been rather less serious than this, because the bishop later regained both his sight and his speech, which the saga naturally attributes to a miracle. But such an assault on a leading churchman was bound to provoke a reaction, and we need to go back two decades or so to understand why Harald might have taken such a risk. There had been a Scottish bishop in Caithness since 1145, but the previous incumbent, Andrew, spent most of his time at the Scottish court and may never have visited Thurso at all. He did, however, support a new tax introduced by Earl Harald which was intended for the support of the Church, and seems to have been the equivalent of the contemporary English 'Peter's Pence'. His successor, John, tried to abolish this tax; his motives for doing so are obscure, but it is of course possible that the Church never actually saw any of this money, which instead went to swell the coffers of the earl. Pope Innocent III eventually intervened and instructed the bishop of Orkney to prevent John from interfering, but the affair left a legacy of resentment on both sides, no doubt made worse by its implications for the independence of John's diocese. Harald also may have suspected John of spying on behalf of King William.

The next victim of the cycle of violence was Harald's son Thorfinn, who was blinded on William's orders in retaliation for his father's crimes. Fordun adds that he subsequently died of his injuries. The Pope was of course also obliged to punish the attack on his bishop, but Harald managed to shift the blame onto the man who had actually wielded the knife, a certain Lumberd, who was alleged to have acted on the orders of an unnamed officer in the earl's army. Lumberd had to perform a painful and humiliating penance, after which he was exiled to the Holy Land for three years. We might wonder whether Innocent, who knew that John had tried to cut off a source of income for the Church, was quite as furious about what had happened as it first appeared. But William the Lion now had another pretext for intervening in the north, and he took full advantage of it. Immediately after Christmas – a season which was normally regarded as quite unsuitable for campaigning in these regions – he raised a huge army and led it into Caithness. For an idea of how this feat of logistics was achieved we can turn to Froissart's account of Scottish tactics in the fourteenth century. Almost every soldier except the very poorest, he says, was mounted on hackneys or ponies, which might have been too small for a mounted charge but were capable of carrying their riders at speed over rough terrain and required no supplies of forage, simply being turned out to graze wherever the army halted. The men themselves were scarcely more demanding, as they needed only a sack of oatmeal and a large flat stone to bake it on (and even the stone could have easily been obtained locally in Caithness). For meat they levied or looted cattle along the way, boiling the flesh in the hide of the slaughtered beast. They could therefore travel unencumbered by baggage and requisition enough food for their needs even in the most inclement season. *Orkneyinga Saga* says that the Scottish expedition filled the entire valley when it camped at Ousdale, near the present border between Sutherland and Caithness, and although we have no exact figures it was certainly big enough to overawe Earl Harald, who was himself capable of mustering as many as 6,000 men. According to Fordun, the exasperated William was also planning to send a fleet to Orkney to cut off his enemy's retreat, but this proved not to be necessary. Instead of fleeing to the islands Harald agreed to submit, pay a large fine and grant the king a quarter of all the revenue from Caithness, after which he was allowed to return home, ruling unmolested until his death in 1206, at which time he must have been around 73 years old.

The end of Norse Caithness

It is not surprising that *Orkneyinga Saga* lists Harald the Old as one of the three most powerful earls that Orkney ever had. He lived in a very different age from his predecessors like Sigurd and Thorfinn, in which the de facto independence of an earldom like Orkney could no longer be taken for granted in the face of increasingly centralised and militarily powerful neighbours like Scotland and Norway, but he had managed to maintain that independence by a mixture of diplomacy, ruthlessness and blatant opportunism. After his death the earldom was ruled jointly by his surviving sons David and John until David's death in 1214, when John became sole earl. In 1209 a large fleet arrived from Norway to reestablish the authority of Sverrir's successor Ingi over both Orkney and Man, and in 1214 William the Lion travelled north again and made a peace treaty with Earl John. At the same time, however, William (and after his death in December 1214 his successor, Alexander II) was pursuing a policy of detaching Sutherland from Caithness and establishing there noble families from further south on whose loyalty they could rely. Sutherland seems until then to have been regarded from a political point of view as part of Caithness, but the people were culturally distinct, speaking Gaelic rather than Norse, and the authority of the earls may always have been tenuous. Now, with Earl John preoccupied with maintaining his father's delicate balancing act between the kingdoms of Norway and Scotland, the latter were quietly chipping away at his mainland territories south and west of the Norse heartland in Caithness. Several charters from the second decade of the thirteenth century (cited by Gray) show that Hugh de Moravia, the grandson of Freskin, the pioneer settler of Moray, already possessed extensive lands along the Dornoch Firth, which he had been granted by King William, and Hugh's son William was subsequently created earl of Sutherland by Alexander. In 1230 we see the first appearance of a subsidiary title, Lord Strathnaver, which was given to the heir of the earls of Sutherland, but it is unlikely that the earls actually exercised much authority over this north-western outpost. According to the traditional history of Clan Mackay (MacDougall, 1953) another new element had already been introduced into the politics of the region when William the Lion exiled a large part of the population of Moray in the 1160s. These refugees are said to have moved north-westwards in search of a place to settle and given rise to the Mackays of Strath

Naver, who in later centuries were to be staunch supporters of the Scottish crown. This story has often been disputed, and the Mackays instead considered to be the descendants of earlier Norse-Gaelic settlers, but Seamus Grannd (2013) considers that their dialect of Gaelic does indeed have affinities with that spoken in Ross or Moray. Whether they displaced an earlier Norse population in the area we do not know, but their presence must have greatly increased the influence of the Scottish kings in the north. Long before that could happen, however, the dynasty of Harald Maddadsson had come to an end.

The final act in their long decline was precipitated by the actions of Bishop John's successor, Adam, in 1222. Adam had made himself unpopular by repeatedly increasing the '*teind*' or tithe which the farmers of Caithness paid to the Church in butter and hay. According to the Icelandic *Flateyarbok*, the farmers held a protest meeting on a hill at Halkirk, six miles south of Thurso, which culminated in an attack on the bishop, who was staying at the local church. Messengers were sent to Earl John, who was apparently on his estate nearby, asking him to mediate, but he took no action, as a result of which the angry mob first murdered the bishop's chaplain, then pushed Adam into his own kitchen and set it on fire, burning him to death. The *Melrose Chronicle* and the *Annals of Dunstable* went further in reporting on the crime, alleging that Earl John had actually ordered the bishop to be thrown into the flames. Whatever the truth of this, King Alexander was either genuinely outraged or saw his opportunity to humble the earl once and for all. As soon as the news reached him he marched north with an army. John fled to Orkney, but was quickly forced to come to terms. He had to pay a large fine to Alexander, as his de facto overlord in Caithness, and hand over some of his lands to the church as compensation. Meanwhile, eighty men who were held to be guilty of the murders were delivered to the king, who ordered their hands and feet to be cut off and their lands confiscated. John had retained his earldom, but no one could any longer doubt where real authority lay. Eight years later a dispute arose over the succession to his territory in Orkney, and in the autumn of 1230 the rival party attacked the house in Thurso where John was staying. They found the earl hiding behind a barrel in a cellar and stabbed him to death. King Haakon summoned the perpetrators to Norway for trial and several were executed, but an even worse disaster occurred when many of the leading men of Orkney, who had travelled to Norway to make their peace with the king, were drowned in a shipwreck on the way home. With no surviving heir to the murdered John, the earls of Angus in Scotland put forward a claim to the earldom through a female line, perhaps that of John's daughter (Crawford, 2013). So the new ruler of Orkney and Caithness was Magnus II, son of the earl of Angus, and despite his Norse name a Scottish nobleman by birth and upbringing. The province's ambivalent position between the two kingdoms was to remain unresolved until 1266, when the Norwegians withdrew all claims to territory on the mainland and Caithness passed permanently under Scottish control.

Visiting the sites

Thurso is easily accessible by both road and rail from Inverness. Harald's Tower (grid reference ND135692) is clearly visible from the sea front at Thurso, and an even better view can be obtained from the ferry which runs between Scrabster in Caithness and Kirkwall in Orkney. It is possible to get close to it on minor roads and tracks, but the monument itself is situated in the middle of a private field and there is no easy access. Technically it can be visited under Scotland's 'freedom to roam' legislation, but the edifice itself is not open to the public and is in a state of some disrepair. The views over the battle site and surrounding country from the vicinity are, however, well worth the trip. The mediaeval Thurso Castle has not survived: the present building on the east bank of the river dates from the nineteenth century, and it is likely that the earlier castle was further to the west. The supposed Dalharrold battlefield is at grid reference NC679390, and can be reached via a track from the car park on the B873 about three miles south of the tiny village of Syre. It is not accessible by public transport, and although there is a memorial which also serves to commemorate the nineteenth-century clearances, there is nothing that sheds any light on the events of our period, especially as the location and even the historicity of the battle are in doubt.

Chapter 8

The End of a Long Struggle: Largs, 1263

Date: 2 October 1263
Location: Largs, Ayrshire
Combatants: King Haakon IV of Norway versus local Scottish
  forces under Alexander of Dundonald, Steward of Scotland
Outcome: Scottish victory

Unlike the other encounters in this book, the Battle of Largs and its location are well known, marked by a monument and a visitor centre, and commemorated by an annual Viking Festival with reenactments and a fair. The battle is included here because it completes the story with which we began, of the struggle between Norsemen and Scots for control of the northern and western coasts, but just as with places like Burghead and Clairdon, an examination of the local terrain and the surrounding countryside can still shed new light on much that is controversial. The campaign had its origin in the process which we have already witnessed in previous chapters, by which the kings of Scots steadily extended their power over the Western Isles as well as mainland districts like Caithness, which had once been firmly in the Norwegian orbit.

Alexander II, who succeeded William the Lion in 1214, had effectively secured Caithness by the 1230s, and was able to turn to his long-held ambition of extending his realm still further to include the Hebrides. In 1249 he led an army into the Isles, allegedly stating that he intended to conquer all the Norwegian territory west of Thurso. He held negotiations with Somerled's great-grandson Ewan

MacDougall of Argyll, who had taken to styling himself 'lord of the Isles' after the death of Harald Olafsson, king of Man, in the previous year. In return for surrendering four castles and pledging allegiance to Alexander Ewan was promised extensive lands in Scotland, but he would only agree if four Scottish earls guaranteed his safety, which suggests that he suspected the king's offer of being a ruse. Matthew Paris reports that three saints, Columba, Olaf of Norway and Magnus of Orkney, were so outraged by Alexander's attempt to disinherit Ewan that they appeared to him in a dream to warn him to call off his campaign, but the king ignored the warning. Consequently the saints cursed him and he died suddenly on the Isle of Kerrera off the coast of Argyll, opposite the spot on the mainland where the town of Oban now stands. His successor, Alexander III, was only seven years old, and for the next twelve years Scotland was in the hands of a succession of regents. Nevertheless, despite this fortuitous breathing space Ewan of Argyll was remarkably unsuccessful in maintaining his freedom of action and his pro-Norwegian stance. In 1250 he attempted to take over the Isle of Man, but was driven out. He then went to Norway to request King Haakon IV to recognise him as king of the Isles, but this was refused. Instead Haakon seems to have reserved the title to himself, in the Latin form 'Rex Insularum'. As Professor Cowan (2017) points out, this was an unequivocal statement of his attitude towards the Scottish claims, and in the long run made war virtually inevitable, as it meant that he could hardly fail to defend the Hebrides if he wished to maintain his credibility.

Haakon's Saga and its author

The main source for the ensuing war is *Haakonarsaga*, the saga of King Haakon, or 'Haakon the Old' as he had come to be known by the final decade of his reign. He had been on the throne of Norway since 1217, when he was only thirteen years of age. The story of how this document came to be written is an interesting one in itself. It begins with the great Icelandic scholar Snorri Sturlason, author of *Heimskringla*, who was assassinated at his home in Iceland in 1241. Snorri was an outspoken opponent of Icelandic union with Norway, a policy which Haakon was pursuing at the time, and which was eventually to be realised a year before the Battle of Largs. However, Snorri had made the additional mistake of speaking out in support of a nobleman named Duke Skuli, who had been regent during Haakon's minority but had risen in revolt against the king in 1239. Skuli was seen as a defender of the old order, under which the king owed his authority to the consent and support of the landowning barons, in contrast to Haakon's 'modern' policy of centralising power in his own hands in alliance with the Church. The Duke was defeated and killed, and Haakon summoned Snorri Sturlason to Norway to explain his attitude. Snorri refused to go, and soon afterwards was murdered by one of his Icelandic enemies, a certain Gissur Thorvaldsson. Few people doubted that the murder had been instigated by Haakon, and when Snorri's nephew Sturla Thordarson came to write his *Islendinga Saga* – an account of the civil wars in thirteenth-century Iceland – he stated this as fact. Consequently, when Iceland came under the Norwegian crown in 1262, its parliament considered Sturla to be a potential troublemaker and exiled him to Norway, where they probably expected him to meet the same fate as his uncle.

But when Sturla reached Norway he found that Haakon had already left on his expedition to Scotland, leaving the country in the charge of his son Magnus. The latter was at first unsure what to do with his unwelcome guest, but Sturla was a professional storyteller and soon made himself popular at court with his recitals. Realising that his life might depend on his skills, and perhaps recalling the tale of the skaldic poem known as the 'Head Ransom' with which the tenth-century saga hero Egil Skallagrimsson had saved his life by flattering King Eirik Blood Axe, the Icelander went on to produce poems in praise of both Magnus and his father. These made such an impression that Magnus commissioned him to write an official biography of King Haakon. Sturla never met Haakon – perhaps fortunately for him, because the king had not approved the project and might still have executed him – but he did interview veterans of the Scottish campaign when they returned. Naturally he was obliged to go to great lengths to avoid criticising Haakon, and had access only to the Norwegian side of the story, but his reliance on eyewitness accounts makes the saga an unusually vivid and valuable source. Sturla went on to have a successful career as lawman, or chief judge, of Iceland under King Magnus, and wrote the new royalist constitution known as Jarnsida. He died, apparently peacefully, in 1284.

Countdown to war

Meanwhile, under an agreement brokered by Henry III of England in 1255, Ewan MacDougall had agreed to transfer his allegiance to the young Alexander III. In 1261 Alexander took control of the government of his kingdom, and according to *Haakon's Saga* he resumed diplomatic efforts to solve the problem of the Hebrides, but these seem to have been remarkably inept and only had the effect of further antagonising the Norwegians. This may in part have been due to the inexperience of Alexander, who was still only twenty years old. In the summer of that year 'an Archdeacon and a Knight called Missel' arrived at Haakon's court, but failed to convince the king of their integrity, and then committed the diplomatic faux pas of setting sail for home without requesting his permission. Haakon sent a fast ship after them and brought them back to Norway, where they were obliged to remain over the winter under house arrest, 'because they had gone away without taking leave'. They were released some time in 1262, probably thanks to the intervention of Henry III, who wrote to Haakon that autumn thanking him for his efforts in the cause of peace. In the meantime, however, the Scots had become impatient and launched a brutal attack on the Isles. Desperate messages were soon reaching Norway from the 'kings of the Hebrides', alleging that the earl of Ross and others had invaded the Isle of Skye and committed atrocities, which included the spitting of small children on their spears – ironically a crime which had once been associated with the Vikings. It was also reported that King Alexander had followed his father's example and publicly announced his intention to conquer all of the Western Isles. Haakon responded by giving orders for the mustering of the leidang, the national levy, and the fitting out of a fleet at Bergen. His son Prince Magnus begged to be allowed to lead the expedition, but the king insisted on doing so himself, arguing that he was older and more experienced, and was more familiar with the 'western lands' which were his objective. Instead Magnus was left to rule the kingdom in his father's absence.

Haakon in 1262 was at the height of his power, and from a Norwegian perspective it must have seemed very foolish of the Scots to challenge him. Greenland came under Norwegian control in that year, as a result of which Sturla was to describe him as the first king to rule north of the Arctic Circle. When the king set sail the negotiations which were to lead to Iceland joining the empire were well advanced. Haakon had secured marriage alliances with Sweden, Denmark and Castile, as well as trading agreements with England and Novgorod. Furthermore, the Kingdom of Man, which had been de facto beyond Norwegian control since the time of Somerled, had been brought back into the fold in the 1240s and could be relied on to provide troops for operations in Scotland. We can get an idea of the nature of Haakon's army from the laws governing the recruitment and equipment of the leidang. By the thirteenth century the obligation to serve in the leidang was often replaced by a tax on free farmers which was intended to pay for the provisioning of the army, but the saga tells us that in this case Haakon chose to levy men and ships in the traditional manner, demanding 'both troops and provisions' from all parts of his kingdom. Each farm, or group of smaller farms, was liable to provide a fully equipped soldier with sixteen weeks' provisions; alternatively, a number of farms might be required instead to send a ship and its crew. These men were far better equipped than their predecessors in the first Viking conquests, especially with regard to defensive armour: the 'Konungs Skuggsja' or 'King's Mirror', which was written around 1250 for the education of Haakon's son Magnus, lists as required equipment for those wealthy enough to afford it a padded aketon, mail hauberk, steel helmet, shield, sword and spear. Mounted troops would add an extra sword to be hung at the saddle bow, mail hose, and mail or padded armour for the horses. Two-handed axes are also frequently depicted in art, and may have remained popular with better-equipped Norwegian warriors just as they did among the Scots.

The ships were equally up to date. Haakon's flagship was an enormous vessel with twenty-seven banks of oars, which he had had constructed at Bergen. It was made entirely of oak, which must have been difficult to obtain in Norway, and decorated with gilded dragon heads. Although it is not named in the saga, Professor Cowan has identified this ship with the 'Cross Clinker' which Haakon is said to have designed himself. ('Clinker' referred to the method of construction known today as clinker built. 'Cross', like its common equivalents 'Krist' and 'Maria', was a Christian dedication intended to invoke divine protection.) Sturla says that there were four crewmen to each half bench, which presumably means that the total complement was eight per bench, or 216 men. The Scottish chronicler Andrew of Wyntoun, who wrote in the early fifteenth century, describes the Norwegian ships as having topcastles from which men could shoot missiles down onto the enemy decks, but he is a late and derivative source. If Haakon's ships were equipped with such unwieldy structures it would not be surprising that they proved to be extremely vulnerable to high winds, but thirteenth-century illustrations generally show vessels virtually identical to Viking longships apart from their greater size. Many of the king's company, who accompanied him on this ship, are named in the saga; they include the treasurer and the master of horse, the abbot of Holm, and various chaplains, chamberlains and cup-bearers. These men presumably had duties other than rowing, so it is not clear whether or not they are included in the head count per bench. If not, the total number on board might have exceeded 250.

The advance to Largs

The fleet left Bergen on 4 July 1263, arriving at Bressay Sound in Shetland after two nights of sailing. It waited there for two weeks before moving on to the sheltered anchorage of St Margaret's Hope on South Ronaldsay in Orkney, from where Haakon sent ships to summon King Magnus of Man to join him. The Manx ships, like the Hebridean galleys, seem to have been smaller than those of the main Norwegian fleet, since those that Magnus subsequently provided to Alexander of Scotland are described by Bower as 'galeis piraticis', or 'pirate galleys', of between twelve and twenty-four oars each. Haakon also sent men to Caithness, where Sturla tells us that the people 'ransomed their lives', or in other words bought him off, but Earl Magnus of Orkney neither joined the king nor provided any troops. No doubt, as Barbara Crawford points out, the Caithness people might have been 'terror struck' by the presence of Haakon, as Sturla claims, but they dreaded the wrath of Alexander even more. The sagas also say that Haakon wanted to send ships to ravage Moray, but had to abandon the idea when the crews refused to be separated from the main fleet. From the outset, then, the campaign revealed unsuspected weaknesses in Haakon's position. Not only could he not rely on reinforcements gathered in Scotland, but even the troops from Norway were not always obedient to his orders. On 10 August the fleet left Orkney and sailed round Cape Wrath to Lewis and then Skye. The news now reached the invaders that Ewan MacDougall of Argyll had taken the Scottish side, but other Hebridean chiefs remained loyal, and one of them, Dougal MacSorley, guided Haakon through the difficult passage round the Ardnamurchan Peninsula and through the Sound of Mull to Kerrera. There what Sturla calls 'outlawed princes', presumably local warlords opposed to the King of Scots, brought their ships and armed men to swell the invading fleet. Haakon met personally with Ewan MacDougall on the Isle of Gigha and tried to persuade him to change sides again, but Ewan refused and the king seems to have had no means of compelling him. He held him captive for a while and then released him with instructions to try and negotiate a truce with Alexander. Haakon also sent raiding parties under the command of Dougal MacSorley and Magnus of Man to harry Kintyre and Bute, where they temporarily occupied Rothesay Castle opposite the mouth of the River Clyde, and encouraged Angus of Kintyre and other local chiefs to bring in some reluctant recruits.

The main aim of the invaders at this point, however, seems to have been to use the threat of invasion to bring about a negotiated peace. The fleet moved on again to Arran, from where a delegation led by the bishop of Orkney was sent to meet with Alexander at Ayr, but talks broke down over the Scots' refusal to surrender the islands which commanded the entrance to the Firth of Clyde: Bute, Arran and the Cumbraes. These must technically have been included in 'the Isles' as defined after Magnus Barelegs' campaign of 1098, but it is not known whether they had ever actually been under Norwegian control. A second attempt at peace-making fell through when the Norwegians took offence at the low rank of the Scottish 'knights and monks' sent to meet their ambassadors. Sturla concluded that it was in the interests of the Scots to delay matters while they raised an army, and there was always the possibility that Haakon would be forced to abandon the campaign, 'for the summer was then passing, and the weather was getting worse'. Haakon responded to the breakdown of talks by sending one of the members of his household, Iver Holm, with another raiding party of Norwegians, Hebrideans and men from Man up Loch Long and overland to Loch Lomond. From a temporary base there they ravaged the countryside and roamed, in Sturla's words, 'almost across Scotland'. An indication that they did indeed penetrate almost as far as the east coast comes from a record in the Exchequer Rolls that men were paid to stand guard at Stirling Castle 'at the time the King of Norway was in these parts'. It has been suggested (Cowan, 2017) that a principal target of the raids was the territory occupied by the increasingly powerful Stewart family, whose growing influence with the king had antagonised the Hebridean warlords since the days of Somerled. Meanwhile the main Norwegian fleet made one more advance to anchor off the Cumbrae Islands opposite Largs on the Ayrshire coast. This was another centre of Stewart power, although it is not known whether this was a factor in Haakon's decision to threaten the area, or whether he was simply hoping to increase the pressure on the Scots by mounting a closer blockade of the shipping route up the Firth of Clyde to Glasgow.

The Battle of Largs

By now a Scottish army was converging on the coast, and as the Scots had perhaps predicted, the weather was taking precedence over politics. On the Monday night after Michaelmas (2 October) a tremendous storm blew up, 'with hailstones and rain', so violent that the saga reports that many believed it was caused by magic. The *Melrose Chronicle* also mentions the storm, drawing the conclusion that it was divine intervention and not human power that frustrated Haakon's ambitions. This is of course a frequent theme in mediaeval historical accounts, but, as Professor Cowan points out, the Norwegians were expert seafarers and well used to storms, so this one must have been truly exceptional if they had to resort to the supernatural to explain it. During the night a transport vessel was driven into the king's ship, entangling its rigging and fouling its anchor. Haakon ordered the transport to be cut loose and it drifted away northwards up the Fairlie Roads, the mile-wide channel between Great Cumbrae and the mainland. In the morning the king was able to row to the island to hear Mass in the church there, but the wind continued to increase until most of the fleet was being driven up the channel. Haakon's flagship went with them, and was not brought to a halt until eight anchors had been put out. It could now be seen that the errant transport, along with a number of smaller vessels, had gone aground on the mainland near the Bay of Largs, and that the crews were being subjected to a hail of missiles from Scottish troops on the shore. They were defending themselves bravely, using the ships as cover, but many were nevertheless being wounded. As the wind was now abating, Haakon sent in some ships to rescue them, and soon afterwards followed in person in a barge. It was now getting dark and the Scots retired before the Norwegian reinforcements, though not before they had thoroughly looted the beached transport.

Norwegian troops continued to land during the night, until by morning there were eight or nine hundred of them. Two hundred of these, under the command of a famous warrior named Ogmund Kraekidants (a name variously translated as Crouch Dance or Crow Dance) – presumably the first wave sent in the previous evening – were holding a position on top of a hill a little way inland, while the rest remained on the beach. It is not clear exactly where Ogmund's men were deployed; Cowan suggests that they were on an eminence known as The Knock, but this is at least two miles north of Largs, and it is hard to see what they would have hoped to achieve by advancing so far ahead of the main army. It is also clear from the saga that the men on the beach were close enough to see when Ogmund came into action against the advancing Scots, which would have been unlikely if the engagement had taken place as far away as The Knock. In fact the Bay of Largs is almost entirely enclosed on the landward side by hills, any one of which might have been the height in question. In any case, the morning light revealed the advance of the entire Scottish army, of which the Scots driven off the previous evening had been only an advance party.

Sturla says that the enemy were 'so numerous that they supposed the king of Scotland was present', but it seems that Alexander was not in fact there, since the main Scottish source, the *Melrose Chronicle*, does not mention him. From contemporary records of payments made to soldiers mustered at Ayr it has been deduced that the army was raised there and marched to Largs from the south. The raising of the troops was therefore presumably the responsibility of the sheriff of Ayr, and we know that they included 120 'sergeants' under Walter Stewart, earl of Menteith, but the overall commander was apparently another member of the Stewart family, Alexander of Dundonald, the steward of Scotland, whose power base was also in the region of Ayr (Barrow, in Reid, 1990). Professor Cowan estimates the total strength of the army as no more than 1500. The *Melrose Chronicle* describes the Scottish forces as 'pedisequi patrie', a phrase which might be translated as 'footsoldiers of the locality'. Professor Barrow argues that the term 'patria' was normally used in this period to mean the local countryside rather than the nation as a whole, which implies that the infantry at least were raised from local estates in places like Strathgryffe, Kyle and Cunninghame. All of these areas were in the immediate hinterland of Largs, and the first two were in the hands of members of the Stewart family. There were also some mounted knights with the army, but it is not known how many: *Haakon's Saga* claims that there were 'nearly five hundred', all riding horses armoured in mail, some of which were expensive Spanish steeds. As discussed in Chapter 1, however, it is unlikely that there were that many knights in the entire Scottish kingdom at that time. In any case an examination of the steep slopes surrounding Largs will quickly dispel any notion of a massed cavalry charge, even if the Scots had possessed the necessary numbers. The infantry are described as using bows, Irish axes and spears, and on occasion as throwing stones. The oral tradition of Clan MacLean would later trace their descent from a warrior known as Gilleathan na Tuaighe, or Gillean of the Axe, who probably held land in south-west Scotland and was said to have distinguished himself fighting on the Scottish side at Largs. Another story, that Gilleathan was once lost on a mountain while hunting and found by his friends who saw the head of his axe protruding above the heather, suggests that the weapon with which he was associated was of the long-handled, two-handed type. (MacLean, 1879). Gerald de Barri describes in his *Conquest of Ireland* how in a battle in 1169 Irish soldiers armed with axes followed behind the first attacking wave and beheaded those enemies who had been knocked to the ground by the charge of the cavalry, but we do not know whether such cooperation between the two arms was practised by the Scots, or whether the horse and foot charged mixed up together or even fought entirely separate actions. The impression given by *Haakon's Saga* is that the Scottish onslaught was launched in haste rather than being carefully planned. The mention of stones in battle accounts might imply the use of slings, but it is equally possible that men simply picked up stones from the hillsides and threw them by hand. Largs was fought not much more than thirty years before the battles of Stirling Bridge and Falkirk, in which the famous 'schiltrums' of close-packed Scottish infantry armed with long spears make their appearance in history, but we have no evidence of such tactics here.

Haakon was still on the shore when the Scots advanced, and according to the saga he intended to remain there and take command, but was reluctantly persuaded to return to the fleet in order to despatch reinforcements. By this time Ogmund Kraekidants was coming under attack in his exposed position by Scottish infantry who pelted his men with stones, forcing them to take cover behind their shields. According to Sturla another nobleman, Andrew Nicolasson, advised Ogmund to retire in order to avoid being cut off, but to do so slowly and in good order. Unfortunately this proved to be impossible, and panic seems to have set in as the Norwegians scrambled back down the slippery hillside towards the beach. Some of the men in the main body also panicked and took cover behind the ships drawn up on the beach, while others tried to escape in boats, several of which sank under the weight of the men trying to board them. The battle seemed about to end disastrously for the invaders, but Ogmund, Andrew and a few others made a stand around the ships and held off the enemy for a while. Haakon was now trying to land more troops, but the process was difficult because of the violence of the waves, as the storm was still blowing. At this point one of the king's 'hirdmen' or household warriors, Haakon of Stein, was killed, an event which must have been noted by both sides at the time since both Sturla and Fordun mention it. Also among the casualties mentioned in the saga was a rash young Scottish knight named Piers de Curry, who 'rode more boldly than any other', and seems to have been killed when he advanced beyond the support of his comrades and was ambushed among the ships. When Norwegian reinforcements under the command of Eilif of Nantsdale finally succeeded in getting ashore the Scots seem to have fallen back again, as Sturla describes a protracted skirmish with missiles, including stones. Eventually Eilif rallied his men and led them forward, whereupon the Scots collected their dead and withdrew. Sturla says that more Scots than Norwegians were killed, but casualties cannot have been especially heavy on either side; those mentioned as being taken to Great Cumbrae by Haakon's men for burial comprised only four warriors and three 'pages'.

The Norwegian retreat and the Treaty of Perth

Haakon had no appetite for another battle. He took his fleet back to Cumbrae, where he met up with the contingent which had returned from the raids around Loch Lomond, but they were in no better state than the main fleet. They had lost ten ships in the storms and their commander, Iver Holm, was so sick that he died soon after his return. The next day the king sent men back to the beach at Largs to burn those ships that could not be brought away, then returned to Lamlash Bay off the Isle of Arran to regroup. He had not been defeated militarily, but neither had he made any progress towards defeating the Scots. He must have been in the position of a boxer who has just delivered his best punch, only to see that his opponent has hardly flinched. While he was on Arran a delegation arrived from Ireland, offering a refuge for the fleet over the coming winter in exchange for assistance against the English. Haakon wanted to agree, but Sturla says that all his people were opposed to the plan, and a 'thing' or conference was held, at which the king promised to return to the Hebrides as soon as the winds were favourable. Magnus of Man sailed home with his contingent and the main fleet proceeded first to Islay, where they resupplied themselves by levying a fine of 300 cattle on the inhabitants who had failed to support them during the advance to Largs, and then, surviving another terrible storm en route, anchored off Kerrera. There Haakon hoped to rendezvous with Ewan MacDougall but he never turned up. Finally, accepting that Ewan had now gone over permanently to the Scots, Haakon gave away all his lands to more loyal chiefs – an action that had no practical consequences at all, as Alexander III had now officially recognised Ewan as lord of the Isles. Haakon also gave away the islands of Bute and Arran, among other places which were no longer his to grant. This may indicate that he did not consider that he had suffered a decisive setback and intended to return, but if so he was soon to be overtaken by events. He stopped to take on supplies in Skye, where Sturla says that a group of Scottish prisoners sent ashore to collect some cattle instead attacked some Norwegians who were taking on water and killed nine of them. This may have been the origin of the false claim later made by the MacKenzies of Seaforth – no doubt with the aim of currying favour with the king of Scots – that one of them had killed Haakon himself (Cowan, 2017).

In fact the Norwegian king was still alive, but his health was failing, no doubt undermined by the immense hardships of the campaign. He reached Orkney, but the weather was still atrocious, so he decided to overwinter there rather than risk the passage back to Norway. He died on 16 December 1263, in his lodgings in the bishop's palace in Kirkwall. He was around sixty years old. Haakon was mourned as one of Norway's greatest kings, but the reaction in Scotland was very different. The *Melrose Chronicle* reports that when Alexander received news of the birth of his son and the death of Haakon on the same day, he regarded it as 'a double cause for joy'. According to Sturla's biography of Haakon's successor, *Magnus' Saga*, the surviving commanders of the fleet in Orkney sent ambassadors to Scotland to seek terms, but Alexander sent them packing. He then took his army to attack Caithness, presumably in order to punish the inhabitants who had paid the 'ransom' to the enemy the previous summer. He also took the offensive against those local warlords in the Western Isles who had chosen the wrong side. Fordun says that Alexander Earl of Buchan and William Earl of Mar were sent to the Hebrides, where they hanged some of the chiefs and collected a huge amount of plunder by way of reparations. King Alexander himself set out to deal with the kingdom of Man, riding back from Caithness the entire length of his own kingdom to collect an army at Dumfries in Galloway. King Magnus of Man did not wait to be attacked, but offered to pay homage, agreeing to serve Alexander whenever required with ten ships. Magnus died in the following year, and Man came under direct Scottish rule.

The new king in Norway, Haakon's son Magnus VI, appointed Ogmund Kraekidants as his commander in Orkney, perhaps fearing that the Scots would now attempt a landing in the islands, then despatched another embassy to discuss peace terms. Magnus's first offer, to surrender Arran and Bute, was understandably dismissed, since Alexander was already firmly in control in those islands. But eventually a deal was hammered out, culminating in the Treaty of Perth, which was signed on 2 July 1266. The Norwegians agreed thereby to surrender to the king of Scots 'Man, with the other islands of the Hebrides and all the other islands on the western and southern side of the great sea'. In return the Scots recognised Norwegian control of Orkney and Shetland, and agreed to pay 1,000 marks a year for four years, followed by an annuity of 100 marks a year in perpetuity. Surprisingly the peace held, even though the Scottish kings quietly stopped paying the annuity at some point in the following century. In 1281 Alexander's daughter Margaret was married to Haakon's grandson, King Eric III of Norway. Orkney and Shetland remained Norwegian until they were transferred peacefully to Scotland as part of a marriage arrangement in 1472. The people of Man soon tried to reassert their independence, but were defeated by a Scottish expedition at the Battle of Ronaldsway in 1275, after which the island alternated between Scottish and English rule until Edward III of England finally took control of it in 1346. The Hebrides remained Scottish, although the kings in Edinburgh were never able to impose their authority fully, and the MacDonalds, self-proclaimed lords of the Isles claiming descent from Somerled, were to be a constant source of dissension until the end of the fifteenth century.

However, for the Scottish kingdom the apparent triumph of the Treaty of Perth was the precursor to a series of tragedies. By 1286 Alexander's first queen and all their children were dead, including

Prince Alexander, whose birth had been celebrated after the Battle of Largs, and Margaret, who had died in Norway while giving birth to a daughter, also named Margaret. The king married again, but one night in March of that year, while riding in haste to see his new bride, he was thrown from his horse and fell to his death over a cliff on the coast of Fife. His only surviving heir was his infant granddaughter Margaret, known as the Maid of Norway. Before his death Alexander had planned that she should marry Edward of Caernarvon, the son of Edward I of England, and if this plan had succeeded it might have ushered in a new age of cooperation between Scotland and its two powerful neighbours, England and Norway. But in the autumn of 1290, while on her way to Scotland, the young queen fell ill and died. She was only seven years old and had not even been crowned. The subsequent events are well known: Edward I's intervention in the question of the Scottish succession; the disastrous reign of his puppet John Balliol; the kingdom's resurgence under William Wallace and Robert the Bruce; and more than two centuries of bloody but ultimately indecisive warfare between Scotland and England. It seems fair to conclude, nevertheless, that one factor in Scotland's survival throughout these traumatic centuries was that the northern frontier with the Norwegians, the cause of endless strife since the days of Sigurd the Mighty, was finally at peace.

Visiting the battlefield

Of the battle sites covered in this book Largs is the easiest to identify on the ground. Tony Pollard, in his survey of the archaeology of Scottish battlefields (2012), laments that the site has been 'completely lost' under more recent development, but the town of Largs is at least aware of the existence of a battlefield, and is provided with the memorial, visitor centre and re-enactment events that we have come to expect from such important sites elsewhere in Britain. It is a pleasant seaside town on the Firth of Clyde, easily reached by train from Glasgow via Paisley, or by the A78 coastal road. The famous monument, popularly known as 'the Pencil', overlooks the sea just south of the town centre. There is a small but worthwhile museum just off Main Street. On the other side of Largs, the Vikingar Centre at 40 Greenock Road offers background information and attractions such as a regular film presentation and costumed storytellers. A fifteen-minute ferry voyage from the harbour serves the island of Great Cumbrae, billed as 'the most accessible Scottish island', from which a panoramic view of Largs and the hills behind can be obtained.

The Kings of Scotland, 844 to 1286

Each name is given in the Anglicised form most commonly encountered in modern works, followed by the mediaeval Gaelic version. Some authors render the names instead in their modern Gaelic equivalents, the spelling of which may differ from those given here.

House of Alpin

Kenneth I MacAlpin (Cinaed mac Ailpin), 844–858.

Duncan I (Domnall mac Ailpin), 858–862.

Constantine I (Causantin mac Cinaeda), 862–877.

Aed (Aed mac Cinaeda), 877–878.

Giric (Giric mac Dungail), 878–889. Possibly co-ruler with:

Eochaid (Eochaid mac Run).

Donald II (Domnall mac Causantin), 889–900.

Constantine II (Causantin mac Aeda), 900–943.

Malcolm I (Mael Coluim mac Domnall), 943–954.

Indulf (Ildulb mac Causantin), 954–962.

Duff (Dub mac Mail Choluim), 962–967.

Cuilen (Cuilen mac Ilduilb), 967–971.

Kenneth II (Cinaed mac Mail Choluim), 971–995. Possibly co-ruler with:

Amlaib (Amlaib mac Ilduilb), died 977.

Constantine III (Causantin mac Cuilein), 995–997.

Kenneth III (Cinaed mac Duib), 997–1005.

Malcolm II (Mael Coluim mac Cinaeda), 1005–1034.

House of Dunkeld or Canmore

Duncan I (Donnchad mac Crinain), 1034–1040.

MacBeth (Mac Bethad mac Findlaich), 1040–1057.

Lulach (Lulach mac Gille Comgain), 1057.

Malcolm III 'Canmore' (from Ceann Mor, or 'Great Chief') (Mael Coluim mac Donnchada), 1057–1093.

Donald III (Domnall mac Donnchada), 1093–1094, 1094–1097.

Duncan II (Donnchad mac Mail Choluim), 1094.

Edgar (Etgar mac Mail Choluim), 1097–1107.

Alexander I (Alaxandair mac Mail Choluim), 1107–1124.

David I (Dabid mac Mail Choluim), 1124–1153.

Malcolm IV (Mael Coluim mac Eanric), 1153–1165.

William I 'The Lion' (Uilliam mac Eanric), 1165–1214.

Alexander II (Alaxandair mac Uilliam), 1214–1249.

Alexander III (Alaxandair mac Alaxandair), 1249–1286.

Appendix II

The Kings of Norway, 872 to 1280

lthough the Norwegian monarchy is usually claimed to have existed continuously since 872, the true situation in the early middle ages was often complex, with several monarchs ruling simultaneously, either as co-rulers or in different parts of the kingdom. There were also numerous pretenders to the throne, especially during the period between 1130 and 1240. In addition Norway was at various times part of the Kingdom of Denmark; where a figure in this list also ruled Denmark for at least part of his reign, this has been indicated by a 'D'. Throughout this period the kings of Norway were *de jure* overlords of Orkney and Shetland, and also between 1098 and 1266 of the Hebrides.

Harald I Halfdansson, 'Fairhair', 872–932.
Eric I Haraldsson, 'Bloodaxe', 929–934.
Haakon I Haraldsson, 'The Good', 934–960.
Harald II Ericsson, 'Greycloak', 961–970.
Harald Gormsson, 'Bluetooth' (D), 961–980.
Haakon Sigurdsson, 970–995.
Olaf I Tryggvasson, 995–1000.
Svein Haraldsson, 'Forkbeard' (D), 1000–1013.
Eric Haakonsson, 1013–1015.
Svein Haakonsson, 1013–1015.
Olaf II Haraldsson, 'St Olaf', 1015–1028.
Cnut, 'The Great' (D), 1028–1035 (also King of England 1016–1035).
Magnus I Olafsson, 'The Good' (D), 1035–1047.

Harald III Sigurdsson, 'Hardrada', 1047–1066.

Magnus II Haraldsson, 1066–1069.

Olaf III Haraldsson, 1067–1093.

Haakon Magnusson, 1093–1094.

Magnus III Olafsson, 'Barelegs', 1093–1103.

Olaf IV Magnusson, 1103–1115.

Sigurd I Magnusson, 'The Crusader', 1103–1130.

The next three decades saw the kingdom fragmented between several rival claimants; at one point there were no fewer than five 'kings of Norway' ruling simultaneously in different parts of Norway and its Atlantic possessions. The most important of these from a Scottish point of view was:

Eystein Haraldsson, 1142–1157.

Magnus V Erlingsson, 1161–1184.

Sverrir Sigurdsson, 1184–1202.

Haakon III Sverresson, 1202–1204.

Inge II Bardsson, 1204–1217.

Haakon IV Haakonsson, 'The Old', 1217–1263.

Magnus VI Haakonsson, 'The Law Mender', 1263–1280.

Appendix III

The Earls of Orkney, c.880 to 1231

M any of the dates given here derive from saga evidence and so are only approximate. Owing to the habit of the Norwegian kings of appointing joint earls and temporarily partitioning the earldom, as well as the tendency for rivals for the throne in Norway to promote their own rival nominees, many of the reign periods listed inevitably overlap. Some of the shorter-lived and less effective claimants have been omitted.

Sigurd Eysteinsson, 'The Mighty', c.880–892.

Einar Rognvaldsson, 'Turf Einar', 895–910.

Thorfinn Einarsson, 'Skull Splitter', 910–963.

Ljot Thorfinnsson, c.963–c.980.

Hlodvir Thorfinnsson, 980–991.

Sigurd Hlodvirsson, 'The Stout', 991–1014.

Brusi Sigurdsson, 1014–1031.

Einar Sigurdsson, 1014–1025.

Thorfinn Sigurdsson, 'The Mighty', 1025–1064.

Paul Thorfinnsson, 1064–1098.

Erlend Thorfinnsson, 1064–1098.

Sigurd Magnusson, 'Jerusalem Farer', 1098–1103.

Haakon Paulsson, 1104–1123.

Magnus Erlensson, 'Saint Magnus', 1106–1116.

Harald Haakonsson, 1123–1130.

Paul Haakonsson, 1123–1136.

Rognvald Kali Kolsson, 1136–1158.

Harald Maddadsson, 'The Old', 1138–1206.
Erlend Haraldsson, 1151–1154.
David Haraldsson, 1206–1214.
John Haraldsson, 1206–1231.

The Kings of the Isles and Kings of Man, 1079 to 1265

The title of king of Man was only officially adopted in 1237. Before that date rulers were variously titled kings of the Sudreyar, or kings or lords of the Isles. They enjoyed differing degrees of autonomy from their nominal overlords, the kings of Norway, and did not necessarily control the whole of the Hebrides. After the Epiphany Battle of 1156 Godred Olafsson and Somerled agreed to divide the Isles between them, with Godred retaining the Isle of Man and the northern Hebrides, and the Isles were never successfully reunited.

Godred Crovan, 1079–1094.
Magnus III Olafsson, 'Barefoot', 1098–1103 (direct Norwegian rule).
Lagmann Godredsson, 1103–1110.
Olaf Godredsson, 'the Red', 1112–1152.
Godred Olafsson, 'the Black', 1152–1187.
Somerled, 1156–1164 (partition of the Isles).
Rognvald Godredsson, 1188–1226.
Olaf Godredsson, 1226–1237.
Harald Olafsson, 1237–1248.
Ragnald Olafsson, 1249.
Harald Godredsson, 1249–1252.
Magnus Olafsson, 1252–1265.

Bibliography

Original sources in translation

Gerald de Barri (Gerald of Wales), *The History and Topography of Ireland*, trans. J. O'Meara, London, 1951.

Gerald de Barri, *Expugnatis Hibernica: Conquest of Ireland*, A. Scott & F. Martin trans, Dublin, 1978.

Gerald of Wales, *The Journey Through Wales and The Description of Wales*, trans. L. Thorpe, Harmondsworth, 1978.

John Barbour, *The Bruce* (ed. A.A.M. Duncan), Edinburgh, 1999.

John Froissart, *Chronicles*, trans. G. Brereton, London, 1968.

Njal's Saga (Ed. and trans. R. Cook), London, 1997.

Orkneyinga Saga (Ed. and trans., H. Palsson & P. Edwards), London, 1978.

Secondary sources

G.W.S. Barrow, *Scotland and its Neighbours in the Middle Ages*, London, 1992.

R.J. Berry & H.N. Firth, *Aspects of Orkney 4: The People of Orkney*, Kirkwall, 1986.

D. Caldwell, M. Hall & C. Wilkinson, *The Lewis Chessmen Unmasked*, National Museums Scotland, Edinburgh, 2010.

F. Cannan, *Scottish Arms and Armour*, Shire Publications, London, 2009.

F. Cannan, *Galloglass 1250–1600*, Osprey Warrior series 143, Oxford, 2010.

W. Clark, *The Lord of the Isles Voyage*, Kildare, 1993.

J.S. Clouston, *The Battle of Tankerness*, Proceedings of the Orkney Antiquarian Society, 1927–28.

E. Cowan, 'The Historical MacBeth', in Sellar (Ed), 1993.

E. Cowan, *The Battle of Largs*, Ayrshire Archaeological and Natural History Society, Ayr, 2017.

B. Crawford, *The Northern Earldoms – Orkney and Caithness from AD 870 to 1470*, Edinburgh, 2013.

F. Fraser Darling & J. Morton Boyd, *The Highlands and Islands*, Glasgow, 1964.

C. Duffy, *Fight for a Throne – The Jacobite '45 Reconsidered*, Solihull, 2015.

S. Duffy (Ed) *The World of the Galloglass: Kings, Warlords and Warriors in Ireland and Scotland, 1200–1600*, Dublin, 2007.

W. Fitzhugh and E. Ward (Eds), *Vikings, the North Atlantic Saga*, Smithsonian Institution, Washington DC, 2000.

S.M. Foster, *Picts, Gaels and Scots*, Edinburgh, 2014.

J.E. Fraser, 'Warfare in Northern Britain, c.500–1093', in Spiers et al, 2012.

E. Gilbert et al, 'The Genetic Landscape of Scotland and the Isles', Proceedings of the National Academy of Sciences of the United States of America, September 2019.

S. Grannd, *Gaidhlig Dhuthaich Mhic Aoidh: The Gaelic of the Mackay Country*, Melness, Sutherland, 2013.

D. Grant, *Old Thurso*, Thurso, 1965.

J. Gray, *Sutherland and Caithness in Saga-time*, London, 1922.

P. Griffith, *The Viking Art of War*, London 1995.

J.E. Harting, *British Animals Extinct within Historical Times*, London, 1880.

J. Hunter, *Last of the Free – A History of the Highlands and Islands of Scotland*, Edinburgh, 1999.

K.H. Jackson, *Language and History in Early Britain*, Edinburgh, 1953.

R.A. MacDonald, *The Kingdom of the Isles*, East Linton, 1998.

R.A. MacDonald, *Outlaws of Medieval Scotland – Challenges to the Canmore Kings, 1058–1266*, Edinburgh, 2016.

M.O. MacDougall, *The Clan Mackay*, Edinburgh, 1953.

M. MacGregor, 'Warfare in Gaelic Scotland in the Later Middle Ages', in Spiers et al, 2012.

E. MacKay, *The Romantic Story of the Highland Garb and the Tartan*, Stirling, 1924.

J.P. MacLean, *A History of the Clan Mac Lean*, c. 1879.

G. MacWhiney & P. Jamieson, *Attack and Die: Civil War Military Tactics and the Southern Heritage*, Tuscaloosa, Alabama, 1982.

M. Magnusson, *Haakon The Old – Haakon Who?*, Largs and District Historical Society, 1982.

P. Marren, *Grampian Battlefields*, Aberdeen, 1990.

J. Marsden, *Somerled and the Emergence of Gaelic Scotland*, Edinburgh, 2008.

A.F. Matheson, *Scotland's Northwest Frontier*, Matador Publishing, Kibworth Beauchamp, Leicestershire, 2014.

N. Melville, *The Two-Handed Sword*, Barnsley, 2018.

J. Miller, *The Gathering Stream – The Story of the Moray Firth*, Edinburgh, 2012.

A. Moffat & J. Wilson, *The Scots: A Genetic Journey*, Edinburgh, 2011.

R. Oram, *David I – The King Who Made Scotland*, Stroud, 2008.

T. Pollard, 'The Archaeology of Scottish Battlefields', in Spiers et al, 2012.

N.H. Reid (Ed), *Scotland in the Reign of Alexander III*, Edinburgh, 1990.

S. Reid, *Scottish National Dress and Tartan*, Shire Publications, Oxford, 2013.

D. Rixson, *The West Highland Galley*, Edinburgh, 1998.

A. Ritchie, 'Excavation of Pictish and Viking-age Farmsteads at Buckquoy, Orkney', Proceedings of the Society of Antiquaries of Scotland 108, 1976–77.

J.L. Roberts, *Lost Kingdoms – Celtic Scotland and the Middle Ages*, Edinburgh, 1997.

A. Ross, 'Moray, Ulster and the MacWilliams', in Duffy (Ed), 2007.

W.D.H. Sellar (Ed), *Moray – Province and People*, Edinburgh, 1993.

W.R. Short, *Viking Weapons and Combat Techniques*, Yardley, Pennsylvania, 2014.

H. Soar, *Secrets of the English War Bow*, Yardley, Pennsylvania, 2010.

E.M. Spiers, J.A. Crang & M.J. Strickland (Ed), *A Military History of Scotland*, Edinburgh University Press, 2012.

D. Stevenson, *Alasdair MacColla and the Civil Wars*, Edinburgh, 1994.

M. Strickland, *War and Chivalry*, Cambridge, 1996.

M. Strickland, 'The Kings of Scots at War, c.1093–1266', in Spiers et al, 2012.

M. Strickland & R. Hardy, *The Great Warbow*, Stroud, 2005.

F. Waters, *Guide to Thurso*, Thurso, no date, c.1970s.

G.J. West, 'Scottish Military Music', in Spiers et al, 2012.

G. Williams, *The Viking Ship*, British Museum Publications, 2014.

G. Williams & P. Bibire, Eds. *Sagas, Saints and Settlements*, Leiden, 2004.

Index